Slices

From the curious & controversial to the heroic & hardy

By Duncan Stearn

Slices of Thai History

From the curious & controversial to the heroic & hardy

By Duncan Stearn

DCO BOOKS

Slices of Thai History

First published 2019
DCO Books

This edition published 2019
by Proglen Trading Co., Ltd.
Bangkok, Thailand
http://www.dco.co.th

ISBN 978-616-456-014-7

Cover by GoBold.design (www.gobold.design)

Also by Duncan Stearn

HISTORY

The Ultimate Accolade, NSW Greyhound of the Year Title 1965-1985
Chronology of Southeast Asian History 1400-1996
Bernborough, Australia's Greatest Racehorse
Thailand Timeline 1500-2015

HUMOUR

Pattaya Unplugged
Our Man in Pattaya

AUTOBIOGRAPHY

Pattaya, Patpong on Steroids

Table of Contents

Introduction

I should note from the outset that the articles appearing in this book pre-suppose the reader has at least a basic idea of Thai history. All 35 pieces are essentially stand-alone snapshots of some major events of the last couple of centuries as well as a few more obscure stories. Hence the reader will notice the stories do not appear chronologically since they are meant to be read as vignettes. A reader can pick up the book, flick to any page and start reading a new story without having had to have read any of the previous pieces.

This book essentially began in early 2001 when the *Pattaya Mail* newspaper began publishing the 'A Slice of Thai History' column. Since the column was restricted to around 500 words or so, and there was plenty of history which cried out to be covered in a little greater depth than that, very often the pieces would be broken up into parts and therefore the story continued for a few weeks. Even so, the aim was to make the history accessible and, hopefully, interesting for the non-academic reader.

The column later continued in the *Pattaya Trader* magazine, with the final column being published in November 2012. While more than 100 'slices' appeared in print it would have been too much to put them all together in one compilation, so I've taken what I hope are some of the most interesting for what may turn out to be a first volume. Who knows, a second volume may be warranted later and covering a more extended timeline.

The reader will see no citations and detailed source notes. Instead I have opted for a select bibliography from which the majority of the information for these stories was gleaned. Once again, this is to avoid being viewed as an academic history. I would hope readers who want to know more will be encouraged to look further afield at more specific publications which cover the areas which interest them.

Duncan Stearn
Pattaya, February 2019

Thailand and the start of the Pacific War

It is often erroneously believed the war in the Pacific commenced with the Japanese surprise attack on the United States naval and air force base at Pearl Harbor in the Hawaiian Islands on Sunday 7 December 1941.

The reality is the attack on Pearl Harbor was in fact *preceded* by two events which took place in the early hours of Monday morning 8 December.

The date discrepancy is due to the International Date Line: Monday 8 December being the same time as Sunday 7 December in the eastern Pacific and the United States.

According to the *London Gazette*, possibly the first offensive action of the war in the Pacific took place on 7 December when a Japanese invasion fleet, led by Admiral Kondo, shot down a British Catalina flying-boat in the Gulf of Thailand.

What is not in any doubt is the first major offensive action was a landing by Japanese troops at Kota Baru on the north-east coast of British Malaya at 12:25 a.m. (local time) while the second act was the invasion of southern Thailand at 1:05 a.m. on Monday 8 December, despite the existence of a mutual friendship pact between the two countries. It wasn't until 20 minutes later Japanese planes began bombing the United States Pacific Fleet in Pearl Harbor.

The Japanese military allocated a mere 138,000 men under General's Yamashita and Lida, as well as two air divisions, to the conquest of Thailand, part of Burma, Malaya, and Singapore. The invasion forces were gathered together on Hainan Island in the South China Sea.

The slow-moving troop transports left Hainan under destroyer escort and headed south on 4 December. Admiral Kondo's main force of two battleships and six heavy cruisers followed soon after.

By 6 December, the British in Malaya were aware a large Japanese amphibious force was heading towards the Gulf of Thailand. Bad weather prevented early detection and it wasn't until the late evening of 7 December the Japanese forces were sighted anchoring off Kota Baru.

As early as July 1941, the British War Cabinet in London were painfully aware the Japanese occupation of northern Indochina in September 1940 meant Malaya and Singapore were vulnerable to air attack.

With war almost inevitable the British military command in Malaya, commanded by Air Chief Marshal Sir Robert Brooke-Popham, drew up a contingency plan calling for a pre-emptive strike across the border into neutral Thailand to thwart any Japanese passage through that country. Codenamed Operation Matador the aim was to advance as far as the Kra isthmus and hope to deny the Japanese the use of the Pattani and Songkhla airfields.

In the months leading up to December, the strategic port of Songkhla and a few of the surrounding towns were a hive of foreign activity, filled with both Japanese and British spies. The Japanese posed as merchants, cameras slung over their shoulders as they photographed anything and everything. The British posed as simple tourists, some claiming to be journalists, others lawyers and accountants. It is suggested a couple pretended to be comedians and one, a circus acrobat. While the Japanese took their task seriously, the British 'tourists', most of whom were officers in various Malay-based regiments, treated the excursions as not much more than a lark. Given the relatively small size of the cities and towns and the few hotel facilities, it is no surprise that on a more than a few occasions both Japanese and British spies stayed at the same place.

Politically, Pibul Songgram, the Thai Prime Minister, faced a dilemma. With war between Japan and Britain almost certain and Thailand unlikely to be permitted to remain neutral due to its geographic position, Pibul Songgram knew he could not expect military support from either Britain or the United States.

After Japan moved troops into southern Indochina in July 1941, he declared Thai neutrality. It was, as he well knew, an empty gesture, made more in hope than geopolitical reality. He said the Thai military would resist all incursions by foreign powers and publicly threatened to implement a scorched earth policy to deter invaders.

This was a public reversal of a private statement he made to the Japanese Naval Attaché in Bangkok in late September 1940 that he would not oppose Japanese landings in southern Thailand in return for an agreement on neutrality and a promise to help restore territory lost by the Thais to the French and British in the previous half-century.

Although the Japanese believed they had an agreement- albeit secret- to transit through Thailand unopposed, they nevertheless prepared for a resisted invasion.

Field Marshal Plaek Phibunsongkhram

Pibul Songgram knew the Japanese were too strong for Thailand to hold out for long, and protracted resistance would lead to his removal from power. He was not certain Japan would be victorious against the British and Americans and was therefore reluctant to commit wholly to Japan. It was his aim to see Thailand on the winning side.

With Japanese forces massing at his borders and an invasion force sailing into the Gulf, Pibul Songgram mysteriously left Bangkok and could not be contacted by Japanese officials, who came to ask if he would honour the secret agreement to allow their forces unhindered transit through Thai territory.

The invasion began with amphibious landings at Songkhla, Thepa, and Pattani just after 1:00 a.m. These landings were unopposed, unlike the earlier assault against the British in Kota Baru. By mid-morning, the Japanese had around 60 aircraft, mainly fighters, on the ground at the strategically important Songkhla airfield.

Japanese landings near the mouth of the Chumphon River, Nakhon Sri Thammarat, and Prachuap Khiri Khan were opposed by the Thai military, as was an invasion of the east from Battambang in Cambodia and an air assault against Don Muang airfield. Thai air force planes flew against superior Japanese forces, losing six fighters.

At Prachuap Khiri Khan, some 120 air force personnel battled with nearly 2,000 Japanese troops for control of the airfield. The battle began around 4:00 a.m.

Just over three and a half hours later, Pibul Songgram re-appeared in Bangkok and immediately ordered a ceasefire. For the Prime Minister the tactics of a brief resistance meant he could later claim the Thais had defended their territory against the Japanese but he had reluctantly ordered a ceasefire in order to save the country from destruction.

A telegram ordering a ceasefire and surrender did not reach the defenders at Prachuap Khiri Khan until 30 hours after fighting had begun. By that time, the morning of 9 December, they had lost 42 killed, including two women. Japanese casualties were estimated at around 400, with over 100 being killed.

At 11:00 a.m. on 9 December, General Percival, the British commander-in-chief in Malaya, gave permission to push troops into Thailand. At 3:00 p.m. (other sources say 5:30 p.m.) two companies of the Indian 11th Division crossed the Thai border with the aim of blocking the Japanese advance from Songkhla. It had been hoped the Thais would remain neutral, but they resisted the British advance, sniping at it all the way. The Indians moved on to Sadao, dug in, and waited for the Japanese.

At the same time, an armoured train advanced into Thailand from Pedang Besar, aiming to interdict any Japanese move from Pattani. They destroyed an important bridge and then withdrew.

The British launched an air strike against the airfield in Songkhla, but only one bomber managed to get over the target. The pilot, Flight Lieutenant Arthur Scarf, was wounded, but managed to return to base, crash landing without injury to his crew. He died later in hospital and was posthumously awarded the Victoria Cross, the first of the Pacific War. A second attack against Songkhla by six British bombers saw three shot down.

Around 9:30 p.m. an advance column of Japanese engaged the Indians around Sadao, forcing them to retreat back across the Malayan border. The British destroyed a couple of bridges, but by midnight, the Japanese were crossing the border.

Also on 9 December, Japanese forces moved into Bangkok after an agreement was signed with the Thai government giving them right of passage through the country. A Japanese air group moved into Lopburi, developing the airfield as a fighter base. The Japanese also took over the telephone line between Lopburi and Bangkok as well as the local radio station.

When Japanese planes sank the British warships HMS. *Prince of Wales* and HMS. *Repulse* on 10 December, the die was cast in favour of a Thai alliance with Japan. Pibul Songgram made a secret agreement with the Japanese to commit Thai forces to the invasion of Burma and on 21 December signed a 10-year treaty of alliance with Japan. The Japanese gave an undertaking to help Thailand recover what Pibul Songgram considered lost territory. At his request, the promise was made in an annex to the treaty and not revealed to the public.

Despite the alliance, Pibul Songgram remained reluctant to declare war on Britain and the United States, but Japanese pressure finally compelled him to do so on 25 January 1942. South Africa and New Zealand declared war on Thailand on the same day. Australia followed soon after.

The truth about Siam's offer of elephants to fight for Abraham Lincoln in the American Civil War

When President James Buchanan of the United States penned a letter to King Mongkut (Rama IV) of Siam in May 1859 and included 192 books of US government publications in the accompanying package, the resultant reply from the Thai monarch has led to some misconceptions which continue to this day.

In May 1856 a commercial agreement between the United States and Siam, known as the Harris Treaty, was signed and later ratified by the United States Senate. As a way of further cementing their relations, James Buchanan, then President of the United States, sent King Mongkut a gift comprising 192 books of US government publications. These arrived in 1860, a presidential election year.

Mongkut responded to this gift by sending a sword in a gold scabbard inlaid with silver, a daguerreotype portrait of himself with the future King Chulalongkorn, and a pair of elephant tusks as presents for the American president.

Included in this selection of gifts was a letter, dated 14 February 1861. Mongkut realised the length of time taken by a voyage between Bangkok and Washington DC, and was aware presidential elections had taken place the previous November, so his letter, while addressed to James Buchanan, took account of the fact the latter may no longer have been in office. After the usual salutary greetings, Mongkut notes his receipt of an official letter from President Buchanan, '…to us from Washington dated at Washington 10th May Anno Christi 1859 which was Wednesday 10th night of Waxing moon in the Lunar month of Visakh, the 6th month reckoning from the commencement of the cold Season in the Year of Goat- 1st Decade of the Siamese Astronomical Era 1221, with a package of Books…'

Mongkut then goes on to make the point the reply is made to Buchanan 'or to whomsoever the people have elected anew as Chief ruler in [his] place …'

King Mongkut, Rama IV

The letter and the gifts were entrusted to a Captain Berrien of the USS *John Adams,* which had paid a courtesy call on Bangkok on behalf of the US government.

Mongkut notes, 'During the interview in reply from Captain Berrien to our enquiries of various particulars relating to America, he stated that on that continent there are no elephants. Elephants are regarded as the most remarkable of the large quadrupeds…so that if any one has an elephants' tusk of large size, and will deposit it in any public place, people come by thousands crowding to see it…

'Having heard this it has occurred to us that, if on the continent of America there should be several pairs of young male and female elephants turned loose in forests where there was abundance of water and grass in any region under the Sun's declinations both North and South called by the English the Torrid Zone- and all were forbidden to molest them; to attempt to raise them would be well and if the climate there should prove favourable to elephants, we are of opinion that after a while they will increase till there be large herds as there are on the Continent of Asia until the inhabitants of America will be able to catch them and tame and use them as beasts of burden making them benefit to the country.'

The letter went on to extol the benefits of elephants to the construction of roads and stated Mongkut would be happy to send the animals to the United States if they so desired, but Siam did not have the means to be able to convey the beasts. He therefore asked that if 'the President… and Congress who conjointly with him rule the country see fit to approve let them provide a large vessel loaded with hay and other food suitable for elephants on the voyage, with tanks holding a sufficiency of fresh water, and arranged with stalls so that the elephants can both stand & lie down in the ship- and send it to receive them. We on our part will procure young male and female elephants and forward them one or two pairs at a time.'

By the time the gifts and the letter offering the elephants arrived in the United States, Abraham Lincoln was President. His reply to King Mongkut was a masterpiece of diplomatic tact and courtesy. 'Your majesty's letters show an understanding that our laws forbid the President from receiving these rich presents as personal treasures. They are therefore accepted in accordance with Your Majesty's desire as tokens of your good will and friendship for the American People…'

Lincoln went on to address the offer of elephants, diplomatically stating, 'I appreciate most highly Your Majesty's tender of…a stock from which a supply of elephants might be raised on our own soil. This Government would not hesitate to avail itself of so generous an offer if the object were one which could be made practically useful in the present condition of the United States.

'Our political jurisdiction, however, does not reach a latitude so low as to favour the multiplication of the elephant, and steam...has been our best and most efficient agent of transportation in internal commerce.' Basically, thanks, but no thanks.

For some strange reason, the contents of the original letter have been distorted to the extent there has arisen a belief King Mongkut did indeed send a herd of elephants which were received and kept by James Buchanan as pets, while others are under the impression Mongkut's offer was made direct to Abraham Lincoln suggesting elephants could be used to help the Union in its struggle with the Confederacy following the outbreak of the American Civil War in 1861.

In fact, no elephants ever left the shores of Siam for a life of free ranging in the forests of the United States, and most assuredly the offer was initially made to President Buchanan with the reply coming from his successor President Lincoln. King Mongkut's offer was made prior to the outbreak of the American Civil War and the letter therefore contains no suggestion of any elephants being used for the purposes of war. An intriguing story, but a myth nonetheless.

'Naga' photograph proved a brilliant exercise in how to market a myth

Sometime in the late 1990s street vendors and shop owners all over Thailand began displaying and selling an impressive photograph which described the capture of a mythical Naga by men of a United States military unit operating at the Mekong River during the Vietnam War.

Queen of the Nagas captured in the Mekhong?

The Naga is a serpent, or water spirit, steeped in Buddhist mythology. Carvings in stone and wood can be seen in many Buddhist temples all over Thailand. Naga are believed to inhabit the murkier reaches of the Mekong River as mythology suggests this is where the centre of the kingdom of the Naga is located. Every year, in late October or early November, people gather along the shores of the Mekong to watch a phenomenon called the Naga fireballs. Many locals believe the fireballs are caused by lurking but unseen Naga.

The caption on the photograph was intended, of course, to convey a statement of either incontrovertible or difficult to ascertain fact. It read, in poor English: *'Queen of Nagas seized by American army at Mekhong River, Laos Military Base on June 27, 1973 with the length of 7.80 metres.'*

Rumours quickly spread that the American soldiers seen holding the Naga all died after eating the flesh of the dead creature. Another rumour claimed the plane carrying the carcass of the dead Naga back to the United States crashed.

It wasn't long before the photograph could be found hanging on the walls of guesthouses, small-scale hotels, noodle shops and ordinary homes as well as being offered for sale to tourists and locals. Just who first found the photograph and hit upon the idea to market it in the fashion they did has never been discovered.

Naturally enough it wasn't long before some people became sceptical about the photograph, doubting its authenticity and believing it to be a good example of the art of photo manipulation. In fact, the suspicion regarding the photograph was wrong on one count, but correct on another.

The date and location of the alleged capture of the Naga were immediately suspicious to anyone with a reasonable working knowledge of the United States involvement in the Vietnam War as it pertains to Thailand and Laos.

The Paris Peace Accords had been signed in January 1973 and by March that year all US combat forces had been removed from Vietnam. There were no US Marine Corps personnel north of the Sattahip naval base at that time, and the closest bases with US troops were in Udon Thani and Nakhon Phanom. There had never been a US military base on the Laotian side of the Mekong, although the base at Nakhon Phanom in the extreme north-east was just across the Mekong from Laos. Known as the 'City of Hills' the Americans nicknamed it 'Naked Fanny' because it was so close to Laos. They called it 'the worst base we had in Thailand, but the best one we had in Vietnam'.

Some sceptics pointed out US forces had not been issued with the style of brown t-shirts shown being worn by the soldiers in the photograph as early as 1973. The background of the picture clearly shows a secure military base with aluminium fencing topped by barbed wire with a US Navy sailor in a white cap.

The real story behind the photograph is far more prosaic. First of all, the photograph is indeed genuine, but is of an oarfish, a creature rarely found alive and rarely seen. The precise photograph of the oarfish being passed off as a Naga was first published in an issue of an American magazine called *Ocean Realm* in late 1996. The same picture was reproduced again in the April 1997 edition of the US Naval publication *All Hands*.

In an article written by William Leo Smith for *Ocean Realm,* he stated instructors with the US Navy SEALS had found the body of an oarfish measuring almost eight metres in length washed up on the shore at a place called Coronado in California while they were out for a morning jog.

The Navy 'notified the Birch Aquarium at Scripps Institution of Oceanography [who sent three people] to the Naval Special Warfare Command…' They looked at the specimen, took a few photos in situ on the beach and interviewed the SEAL instructors who found the fish. The scientists could not find any 'obvious reasons for death…Externally, the fish had a few large gashes on its right side…behind the head, and a noticeable piece of the forehead had been removed as well.' They surmised the oarfish's '…wounds were caused by a propeller of some sort.'

The body of the oarfish was brought back to the Naval Special Warfare Command base where it was washed off and pictures were taken of the 100 kilogram-plus creature, 'with different Navy personnel.'

The article noted, 'Oarfish tend to be more tropical species…However, they are found worldwide…predominantly in the tropics.' Little is known about the oarfish although it is known they are not good for eating. Some scientists baked a piece of the fish and said it shrank a lot and tasted like fibrous paper.

Local ingenuity, a dash of the mystical and eerie, and some clever marketing all combined to create one of the most recognisable pictures of late twentieth century Thailand.

The day Siam recognized the Republic of Slovakia...six decades early

When a letter written on parchment-like paper and bearing a large cerise seal arrived at the Foreign Ministry in Bangkok in early 1929, Thai officials naturally handled the missive with great care. Once the contents had been translated, officials noted that it requested the Royal Siamese Government formally recognize the new Republic of Slovakia.

King Prajadhipok, Rama VII

The letter was signed by a Professor Mihalusz, who claimed to be the new President of the Republic of Slovakia, with its capital at Trencsen (modern day Trencin). Naturally, King Prajadhipok (Rama VII) and his senior advisers, led by 46-year-old Foreign Minister

Prince Traidos Prabandh (a former Siamese ambassador to the United States), deliberated on the request. Clearly Slovakia had successfully seceded from Czechoslovakia, which had been created just a decade earlier at the conclusion of the First World War from the charred remains of the old Austro-Hungarian Empire.

Since the President of Czechoslovakia was Professor Masaryk, the Thai ministers came to the conclusion the Slovakian secessionists had also chosen a professor as their first elected leader.

A few weeks later the postmaster in Trencsen received a letter emblazoned with the Royal Coat of Arms of Siam and addressed to His Excellency the President of Slovakia, Professor Mihalusz. The postmaster went post haste to see the mayor. He opened the letter and read with mounting concern the contents in which His Majesty King Prajadhipok declared himself graciously and inexpressibly pleased to accord full recognition *de facto* and *de jure* to the Sovereign Republic of Slovakia.

The mayor of Trencsen quickly drafted a letter to be sent as quickly as possible to Bangkok. He explained Slovakia had not seceded from Czechoslovakia, the capital city remained as Prague and not Trencsen, and the President was still Professor Masaryk and not Professor Mihalusz.

The mayor went on to explain that some time in the early part of 1928 a group of Slovakians held a mass meeting led by Professor Mihalusz, an old botanist of minor renown, at which they issued a 'Declaration of Slovak Independence'. The mayor wrote that the whole exercise was more academic than revolutionary and was easily suppressed by the local police. Professor Mihalusz, obviously frightened by the police interest in him, later fled Trencsen and had not been seen for some time. He was believed to be hiding out in Vienna from where he had probably written the letter that won Slovakia recognition from Siam.

Slovakia eventually achieved independence from Czechoslovakia, in 1993.

The Paknam Incident and its ramifications, 1893

To reach the Bangkok roadstead it is necessary for vessels to sail into the mouth of the Chao Phrya River, and as early as the reign of King Rama II (1809-1824) Thai strategists were aware of the importance of the seaport of Samut Prakan, situated right at the entrance to the river on the Gulf of Thailand. Samut Prakan had been constructed between 1620 and 1628 at the height of the Ayutthaya Period.

In 1819, the king, in conflict with Vietnam and worried about a possible sea borne attack, ordered the construction of six forts in the area around Paknam. Three of the forts were completed over the next three years, while the remaining three were finished during the reign of King Rama III.

Paknam had started as a small fishing village but began to flourish soon after the Thai capital was moved to Bangkok in 1782. All ships coming up the Chao Phrya River had to stop at Paknam to take aboard a customs officer. For a period of time, all ships had to unload their guns at Paknam, before they were allowed to continue on to Bangkok.

To further strengthen the seaward defences, another fort was ordered constructed on the west side of the Chao Phrya River at the entrance to the estuary. This was the Phra Chulachomklao Fort, designed to command the river mouth as well as two kilometres upriver.

Commanded by a Danish captain, the Phra Chulachomklao Fort was only completed early in 1893, right at the time Siam was embroiled in a dispute with France over the sovereignty of Laos.

The French were determined to increase their imperial possessions in Indo-China, a move that naturally brought them into conflict with Siam. France claimed the eastern boundary of their occupied state of Annam (Vietnam) was marked by the Mekong River, whereas the Thais said their eastern border was a 'chain of mountains parallel to the seaboard' (from an editorial in the *New York Times*, 29 June 1893, p. 4)

On 14 March, Monsieur Pavie, the French Charge d'Affaires in Bangkok, was instructed by his government to demand Siam's immediate withdrawal from the left bank of the Mekong River and seek compensation for French subjects whom France claimed had suffered damages. At the time, the French gunboat Le Lutin was anchored in Bangkok, as a visible threat to the Thais.

THE FRENCH WOLF AND THE SIAMESE LAMB.

From Punch magazine

In the meantime, on 3 April a French military column reached Stung Treng, on the Cambodian side of the Mekong River. The 14-man Thai post at Stung Treng retreated without firing a shot. Two days later the French took possession of nearby Kong island. At the same time, King Chulalongkorn made a decision to fight rather than meekly submit to the French and issued orders for three new forts to be built on the Chao Phrya River to defend Bangkok. He also hoped to purchase three warships and expand the army while also sending forces to bolster the garrison at the gulf port of Chantaburi.

Pavie, alarmed by these preparations, advised an immediate resolution of the crisis, not by negotiation but by military action. The French Foreign Minister, Jules Develle, ordered Admiral Edgar Humann, the commander of the French Far Eastern Naval Division, to concentrate his nine warships off Saigon. Pavie, in turn, thought this presented the ideal moment to turn Siam into a French protectorate and thereby 'round off our Indochinese Empire.' (Pavie to Develle, 13 May 1893)

The stakes increased when the Thais regained control of Kong island, capturing a French captain. Then, the French Inspector of the Civil Guard was ambushed and killed. France claimed he had been murdered.

In June the French government reacted by sending Le Myre de Vilers as a special envoy to Bangkok, with instructions to withdraw their entire diplomatic mission and, with the help of Jean de Lanessan, the Governor-General of Indo-China, to send warships to blockade the mouth of the Chao Phrya River if Siam refused to recognise the French claim to the left bank of the Mekong River and pay compensation for a series of incidents stretching back to 1891.

At the same time, worried by the escalation in French demands upon Siam, British Prime Minister Lord Rosebery sent two gunboats to Bangkok, ostensibly to provide protection to British citizens. In reality, as Lord Kimberley, the Secretary of State for India, wrote privately to Rosebery, sending gunboats was 'the natural mode of demonstrating…'

On 10 July, France informed the Thai Foreign Minister, Prince Devawongse, that the French gunboat's Inconstant and Comete would, in accordance with Article 15 of the Franco-Thai Treaty of 1856, cross the bar and anchor at Paknam island before proceeding to Bangkok. Prince Devawongse issued a protest at this intended violation of Thai sovereignty and asked that negotiations take place between the two sides before these warships were dispatched.

Although the French government agreed, Admiral Humann, nonetheless issued orders for the warships to proceed to Bangkok. The French gunboats, with a small French merchant ship, the Jean Baptiste Say as a pilot, sailed towards the entrance of the Chao Phrya River on 13 July.

Thai artillery, installed in the newly constructed Phra Chulachomklao Fort as well as the Phissuasamut Fort, opened fire on the advancing French. Thai gunboats also joined the assault. The

Jean Baptiste Say was sunk and the Thai steel cruiser Makut Rajah Kumar damaged, but the Inconstant and Comete managed to force their way through, sailed up the Chao Phrya and anchoring opposite the French Legation in Bangkok where they trained their guns on the Royal Palace. Two or three French sailors were killed in the action while the Thais lost between 15 and 25 dead.

On 20 July, France issued an ultimatum, with a 48-hour deadline, demanding Siam formally recognise the rights of Annam and Cambodia over the left bank of the Mekong River and the islands in the Mekong River; withdraw Thai troops from the left bank within one month; pay compensation for damage inflicted on French troops and warships; punish Thai offenders and pay compensation to the families of French subjects adversely affected by Thai actions; pay an indemnity of two million francs to French subjects for various claims and deposit the sum of three million francs as a guarantee Siam would abide by these demands.

The French had also occupied the small island of Koh Si Chang, opposite Sri Racha, and on 22 July Admiral Humann arrived to oversee future operations.

Siam was forced to accept the French ultimatum but asked that the rights of Annam and Cambodia over the left bank of the Mekong be limited to the 18th Parallel. The Thais also sought the joint use of the islands in the Mekong. The French rejected the Thai proposals and withdrew all their consular officers from Bangkok and blockaded the Gulf of Thailand, using Koh Si Chang as their headquarters.

The incident caused relations between the two colonialist powers France and Britain to grow tense, although the British were unwilling to risk a war over the independence of Siam, despite the tacit support of Germany. Instead, the British advised the Thai government to accede to French demands in order to avoid an all-out conflict. The Thais conceded and on 3 August, the French lifted their blockade of Bangkok.

Siam subsequently signed a treaty with France on 3 October 1893 by which the Thais renounced their claim to territory on the left bank of the Mekong River as well as the islands in the river; agreed not to construct any fortifications or military establishment within a

40-kilometre radius of the right bank of the Mekong River and gave the French government the right to establish consulates wherever it deemed appropriate, (such as Khorat and Nan). The French also demanded the right to occupy Chantaburi (Chantaboon) until Siam complied with all the terms of the treaty.

The compensation demanded by France amounted to some 3 million francs and was paid for out of Siam's foreign reserves as well as a contribution by King Chulalongkorn and some of his relatives. The silver was delivered to the French gunboat *Le Lutin*, moored in front of the French embassy in Bangkok.

On 4 December, an Anglo-French agreement was signed which ostensibly guaranteed Thai independence. Basically, France and Britain agreed to maintain the region as a neutral zone using the Mekong River as a boundary line. In a subsequent declaration, the British and French agreed not to send troops to the region between the Mekong River and the Tenasserim Mountains without the prior consent of the other party and stated that French and British nationals residing in the region would not receive special privileges or benefits which nationals of the other party did not receive.

The agreement, reached without the involvement of Siam, basically meant that neither Britain nor France would impinge upon Thai sovereignty without the prior consent of the other party. Really, it in no way guaranteed Thai independence, but merely indicated that the British and French were not prepared to go to war over Siam.

France used the registration of French subjects in Siam as a tool to expand her influence in the country. In 1880, only 146 people were registered as French subjects, and 96 of these were Chinese. In reality, the Chinese should not have qualified as French subjects, but the French considered that their employees should also be accorded protection by the French Legation. Even Cambodians, who by the Treaty of 1867 had been placed under the jurisdiction of Thai courts, were registered as French subjects.

Between 1893 and 1896, the number of people qualifying as French nationals grew from 200 to 30,000, with the French Legation actively encouraging all French employees to register as French subjects.

For example, in 1912 the number of Chinese registered as French subjects in Bangkok alone totalled 724. By contrast, only 36 Chinese were registered as British subjects during the same period in Bangkok.

In January 1896, a second Anglo-French agreement regarding Siam was signed. The British abandoned their claims to any territory east of the Mekong River, thereby making the river the official border between Laos and Burma. In return, the French again agreed to accept the independence of Siam.

Cementing relations further with the British, Siam signed a secret agreement with Britain in April 1897 whereby the Thais agreed not to cede any territory or rights south of the 11th Parallel on the Malay Peninsula without prior British consent. In return, Britain promised to support Siam against any attempts by a third power to assume control in the Malay Peninsula.

The French continued to occupy Chantaburi until 7 October 1902 when an agreement was signed between France and Siam by which the latter agreed to cede two southern Lao provinces. However, the agreement was not ratified by the French parliament and French troops occupied Trat.

The seven Armstrong guns that participated in the action against the French in 1893 were still in working order 105 years later when they fired a seven-gun salute to celebrate the fort's anniversary. Since the Paknam Incident, they have never fired a shot in anger.

Sunthorn Phu: Thailand's most famous poet

Born on 26 June 1786 in Bangkok, Sunthorn Phu was to become the poetic voice of the nation, compared by some critics with English great Geoffrey Chaucer. This son of a Rayong native was a contemporary of romantic British poets Percy Shelley and William Wordsworth. Sunthorn Phu is also one of Thailand's most famous alcoholics.

Memorial to Sunthorn Phu at Wat Si Sudaram, Bangkok
Credit Photographer: Heinrich Damm - own work, CC BY 2.0
https://commons.wikimedia.org/w/index.php?curid=782605

The poet was born into humble surroundings and grew up under the reign of King Rama I (1782-1809). His parents divorced soon after Sunthorn Phu was born, his father returning to Rayong and becoming a Buddhist monk. His mother married again and became the wet nurse of a princess in the royal palace, taking her son with her.

His education, as was typical of the time, took place in a monastery, in Wat Sri Sudaram, located on Khlong Bangkok Noi. When he finished his education he became a civil service clerk. His proximity to the royal palace saw Sunthorn Phu conduct an affair with a girl named Chand, a member of the inner court of Rama I. When the affair was discovered, the love-struck elegist and his paramour were arrested and thrown in jail.

They were released in 1806, and Sunthorn Phu decided to visit his father, whom he hadn't seen since his parents had separated. On the way to Rayong he penned the first of his great poems: Nirat Muang Klaeng, in which he described his journey to Rayong and his continuing love affair with Chand.

Sunthorn Phu originally intended to join his father in the monkhood for a term, but soon after arriving in Rayong he fell ill with a fever. He stayed with his father for two months but after recovering from his illness returned to Bangkok.

The budding poet and Chand were granted permission to marry, and soon after a son was born. Sadly, their marriage failed due to the poet's love of alcohol. Chand found another man and left Sunthorn Phu to his booze and poetry.

In 1807, the 21-year-old wrote a poem entitled Nirat Phra Bat. It told the story of his visit to the shrine of Phra Buddha Bat in company with one of Rama I's sons and also referred to the problems that had arisen in his relationship with Chand.

The success of the poem brought him royal patronage. Rama II, himself a poet of acknowledged ability, thought him wonderful and gave Sunthorn Phu a position at court. The King consulted him during the course of writing his own famous work Ramakien. For this help the King gave him the title of Phra Sunthorn Voharn.

Despite this success, the poet couldn't leave alcohol alone and on one occasion he severely injured an uncle who tried to intervene when Sunthorn Phu was arguing with his mother. The King, despite his fondness for the poet, sentenced him to prison.

It was during this prison sentence he achieved eternal fame when he began writing Phra Apai Mani, a very long and adventure-packed poem. The poem, running to 94 books and 30,000 lines of verse, was serialised and became required reading in Thai schools until the late twentieth century. Although it wasn't fully completed for many years, it became instantly popular with readers as it was released in serialised form.

The poem recounted the adventures of two royal brothers, Phra Apai Mani and Srisuwan. Their father, the king, sent the two young princes into the wilderness to seek out teachers and obtain an education. During this period they followed the precepts of ancient Indian tradition and lived lives of austerity with their followers. They returned to their father after seven years, both having excelled at their studies. Apai Mani had learned to play the flute so brilliantly that anyone hearing his magical melodies would fall into a deep sleep. Srisuwan had studied the art of dancing with a pole so skilfully that he could escape anyone who tried to harm him. Unfortunately, their father was displeased with his sons' choice of skills and in a fit of pique banished them from his lands. The brothers wandered the earth for the rest of their days, but the skills they had learned proved invaluable whenever they ran into trouble.

King Rama II granted Sunthorn Phu a full pardon and the poet resumed his position at court as a literary adviser and instructor of the monarch's sons. He was among the literary circle, led by Rama II, who wrote The Story of Khun Changand Khun Pan.

It was while acting as a literary adviser that Sunthorn Phu incurred the wrath of Prince Jesdabodindra, the future King Rama III. The poet publicly criticised some lines written by the heir to the throne, a slight the prince never forgave.

In 1824 Rama II died. The new king immediately withdrew all royal favour from Sunthorn Phu and the alcoholic poet, now aged 38 was forced to join a monastery. He spent the next eight years or so at a temple not far from the Grand Palace before one of Rama III's brothers, Prince Lakhananukhun took a liking to his works and brought him tentatively back into the royal fold. He wrote a few more cantos of Phra Apai Mani and a few other poems before his royal mentor suddenly died in 1835 and once more Sunthorn Phu was cast out into the wilderness.

Oh, how everything was against me then.
Even termites made their way to my bedroom.
They ate the mat and destroyed all my books.
It was distressing to think of those books
And the yellow robes I used to wear
Had holes in them like my weeping eyes.

For the next few years he lived on a small boat and sailed around the khlongs of Bangkok and into the hinterland, writing and trying to sell his works to sustain himself.

The pendulum swung again in Sunthorn Phu's favour when Prince Isaresrangsan, a son of King Rama III, took a liking to him and brought him into his service. When Prince Mongkut ascended the throne as King Rama IV in 1851, Sunthorn Phu's mentor was raised to the rank of His Majesty Phra Pin Klao. He completed the rehabilitation of Sunthorn Phu and made him Poet Laureate, reinstating his title of Phra Sunthorn Voharn. In this final period of his life he wrote another acknowledged fine piece entitled Nirat Phra Pathom.

In 1844, the poet had published a book entitled A Maxim for Ladies, a work offering advice for women on how they should behave. Despite its anachronistic precepts, some of the advice was still considered valuable into the twenty-first century. Some examples of this included, 'Walk slowly…do not swing your arms too much. Do not sway your breasts and do not run fingers through your hair. Do not run after men. Be faithful [and] humble [to] your husband. When [your husband] has aches and pains, massage him, then you may go to sleep. Get up [early] and prepare water for him to wash.'

Despite his alcoholism, Sunthorn Phu lived to the age of 68, dying in 1855. At his passing he left a vast body of work including nine travelling poems, five stories, four lullabies, two song recitals, two collections of proverbs, and one play. Despite his prolific output there are, and were, those who considered his verse merely populist.

Perhaps the piece of poetry which virtually encapsulates the troubled life of Sunthorn Phu was the one he entitled A Poet Can Never Escape Liquor. In just 13 lines it could almost be his biography.

Arrived at a distillery;
A smoking stove and a bucket hung by a rope from a pole
Oh, karma, because of that evil water
I am drunk, mad, shameful.
Let me make merit and achieve enlightenment
So when I am faced with liquor
I'll be saved:
Never to go near it or see it.

But when I'm not drunk on liquor,
I'm drunk on love.
How can that temptation be stopped?
Thc hangover of whisky is gone the next day,
But the hangover of love lasts forever.

His simple language and verse, and sincerity (writing from the heart and not the head), were precisely what appealed to the masses and his turbulent private life just added spice to his allure. In 1986 he was officially recognized by UNESCO.

Siam and the First World War

When Woodrow Wilson, the President of the United States, declared war on Germany in April 1917, it was clear American entry would eventually turn the tide against the Central Powers (Germany, Austria-Hungary, the Ottoman Empire, and Bulgaria).

Watching on the sidelines, King Vajiravudh (Rama VI) considered his options. Siam had remained neutral since the outbreak of war in August 1914, and his nation enjoyed friendly relations with Germany, but Vajiravudh recognised the political value of throwing in his lot with the Allied Powers (Britain, France, Italy, and Japan).

He was convinced participation would be '…an excellent opportunity for us to gain equality with other nations.' Siam had suffered from the imperial designs of the British and French, losing great swathes of territory in the 20 years or so prior to the outbreak of war in Europe.

Additionally, Siam had been coerced into signing agreements accepting the imposition of extraterritorial rights for the citizens of nations such as France, Britain, and the United States, and Vajiravudh hoped Siamese involvement in the war would lead to a revision of these unequal treaties.

Therefore, on 22 July 1917, despite the misgivings of some members of the government, King Vajiravudh instructed Interior Minister Chao Phraya Surasi to declare war on Germany and Austria-Hungary. Among the reasons cited was a claim the Central Powers were 'ignoring the norms of warfare and fighting in an immoral way.' One of Siam's first acts was to intern, and later seize as war reparations, 12 ocean-going ships of the North German Line (NGL) as well as the Bangkok docks and warehouses of the firms Windsor Rose and Markwald.

There was a certain irony in Siam allying itself with France, a nation that had bullied her way into annexing large chunks of Siamese territory over the previous 50 years. Such are the vagaries of geo-politics.

Then again, Vajiravudh had been the first monarch educated abroad, being sent to Britain. He spoke fluent English, had been at

Sandhurst Military College, and commissioned an officer in the Durham Light Infantry. The Anglophile monarch was contrasted by a number of royal relatives who had spent time being educated in Germany. A coup in March 1912 by 92 low-ranking royals, many pro-German, who hoped to replace Vajiravudh, did not pre-dispose the ruler towards Germany or her allies.

Not much happened until 21 September when the king gave the order for Chao Phraya Bodin, the Minister of War, to call for volunteers to make up an expeditionary force to fight in Europe. A limit was placed on overall numbers and an expeditionary force totalling 1,284 men was raised, under the overall command of Major General Phraya Pijaijarnrit (later promoted to Lieutenant-General and known as Phraya Devahastin). Volunteers were divided into three units: motor transport, medical, and aviation.

Thai records suggest the force left Siam on 19 June 1918 and landed at Marseilles on 30 July where the three sections were separated and sent for training in different parts of France. Yet a report sent to the American Consul in Melbourne, Australia on 4 June stated, 'A contingent of Siamese troops has also joined the Allies.' This is a strange discrepancy of almost two months between the Siamese chronicles and a contemporary account.

The motor transport section finally moved up to the Western Front in October 1918. For five days, from 26 October, the Siamese supplied French forces in an area subjected to German artillery fire and later received the Croix de Guerre from the French government as a unit citation.

About 95 air personnel, training at French Army Flying Schools, qualified as pilots, but had not completed their courses when the war ended on 11 November. The motor transport unit went into the occupied part of the Rhineland with French forces following the signing of the armistice.

There is a suggestion the medical unit included nurses, although no concrete evidence of this has come to light, at least in English or French. It is claimed these were the only women to serve in the trenches on the Western Front, but this seems extremely unlikely.

The aviation contingent returned to Siam, arriving in Bangkok on 1

May 1919 while the remainder of the volunteer force landed on 21 September.

The Siamese Expeditionary Force during the 1919 Paris Victory Parade

A now almost-forgotten war memorial was erected in honour of the troops and stands on the edge of the Sanam Luang (Pramane) ground in Bangkok. Called the Volunteer Soldiers' Monument it has inscribed the names of the 19 soldiers claimed as casualties of the conflict, none in battle. The remains of the casualties were interred in the monument on 24 September 1919 but the memorial itself was not officially unveiled until 22 July 1921, a strange and unexplained delay.

Of the 19 names inscribed on the monument, two men in Bangkok before the force left for Europe, presumably during training. Nine died in France and the other eight in Germany. Of these, 10 expired in hospitals or medical stations. Britain, Europe, and much of the rest of the world was gripped by Spanish influenza from the latter months of 1918 until 1920, one of the most virulent epidemics ever known. It is highly probable some of the hospital casualties were caused by Spanish flu. The remaining deaths appear to be the result of vehicular accidents.

Siam also participated in the Versailles Peace Conference with Articles 135, 136, and 137 devoted to her in the final Treaty of Versailles. In January 1920, Siam became a founding member of the League of Nations.

On 1 September 1920, King Vajiravudh's decision to go to war was vindicated when the United States ceded her extraterritorial rights. France, after five years of extensive negotiations, relinquished her rights in February 1925 while Britain signed a treaty to the same effect in July the same year.

Raising the Standard: Thailand's national flags

Thailand's current national flag was first unfurled on 28 September 1917, and was an adjustment to the previous national flag, which had been introduced only a year earlier. The current flag consists of red, white, blue, white and red stripes, the one introduced in 1916 by King Vajiravudh (Rama VI) was even simpler: red, white, red, white and red stripes only.

According to some sources, the king was on a boat trip up the Chao Phraya River when he noticed the-then 61-year-old national flag, at the time a white elephant on a red background, being flown upside down over a hut. It wasn't a good look.

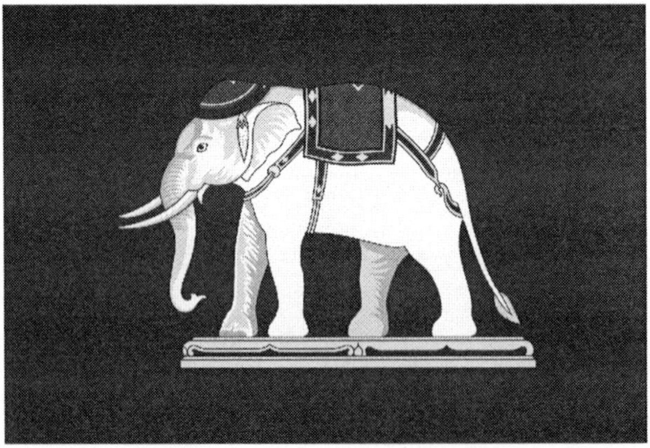

This flag was being used 1916-1917

Considering the flags of most European powers were based on stripes, representing their national colours, Vajiravudh simply followed their line to come up with his original five horizontal stripes of red, white, red, white, and red.

Just why the middle red stripe was changed to blue has never been properly explained. The three-coloured version is known as the 'Trairanga' or 'Trairong', meaning tricolour. The prevailing- although unofficial- view of the meaning of the five stripes is that red represents the land and the people; white is for Theravada Buddhism, the state religion; and the central blue stripe symbolises the monarchy. It has also been stated that blue was the official colour of King Vajiravudh.

Yet another account claims the blue was inserted as a show of solidarity following Thailand's entry into the First World War (in July 1917) as an ally of Britain and France. You would think it couldn't be that hard to work out why the blue stripe replaced the red, but maybe no one bothered writing down the precise reason, thus allowing some variation and confusion to reign.

Most sources seem to agree the first national ensign was a plain red colour with no other markings or features.

The first account to mention any sort of national flag symbol occurred during the reign of King Narai (1656-1688). According to some sources, a plain red banner was displayed by Ayutthayan merchant ships trading with foreign countries.

It is generally believed the first official Thai national flag was unfurled in 1680 when a French warship arrived at the mouth of the Chao Phraya River on a goodwill visit. The local governor was asked by the French commander if it would be allowed to fire a salute as it entered the mouth of the river. Permission was given and the Siamese manning the fort at the entrance returned the salute.

As it was customary to raise the national flag before a gun salute was fired, the governor found a suitable piece of red cloth, attached it to a rope and raised it to accept the French salute. Thai practicality at its best.

Research by Prince Damrong, a brother of King Chulalongkorn, showed the use of the red ensign could certainly be traced to the reign of King Borommakot (1733-1758) and a mission by 18 Buddhist monks who travelled to Sri Lanka in 1752 in an attempt to restore Sinhalese Buddhism. A journal, written at the time, mentions only red flags were used on the Thai sailing vessels.

Some time between 1752 and 1800, the Thai flag may have had a white chakra -a Buddhist wheel, shaped like a fan- added to the plain red.

Then, in 1817, during the reign of King Rama II, a white elephant was added to the centre of the chakra.

An American publication entitled *The Flags of the Principal Nations of the World* (published in 1837) shows the flag of Thailand as red with a white disk in the centre. On the white disk is a drawing of a sun with a face on it. This same drawing appears in renditions of the flags of both Uruguay and Peru.

The flag of Burma (only a part of which was under British control) is rendered as a red field with a white elephant facing the flagpole. This would seem to be more representative of Siam than Burma and almost certainly indicates a mistake made by the editors of the publication. 'The readers won't notice' might have been the thought.

In 1855, during the reign of King Mongkut (Rama IV), the white chakra was dropped and the flag became simply a red field with a white elephant in the centre. This remained the national symbol for the next 61 years, until that fateful day in 1916 when Vajiravudh saw it being flown upside down.

The Invasion of Kedah, 1821

For centuries while Siam paid tribute to China in recognition of Chinese suzerainty, so many of the states in the northern section of the Malay peninsula did the same to the-then kingdom of Ayutthaya and latterly to its successor, based in Bangkok.

Specifically, the Malay sultanates of Kedah (often rendered as Quedah in press reports of the early nineteenth century), Pattani, Perak, and Terengganu would periodically send what was termed the 'Bunga Mas', or Golden Flowers, to the Siamese monarch as recognition of their fidelity. The reality was that Siamese suzerainty over these states was fleeting at best and by the middle of the eighteenth century the rulers of the Malay states considered their relationship with Siam to be one of mutual friendship rather than one of servant and absentee master.

The Sultan of Kedah showed an especially independent nature in his conduct of foreign affairs when, after delicate negotiations, he gave permission for the British East India Company to establish a permanent trading post on the island of Penang in 1786. The Sultan did not consult with his ostensible overlords in Bangkok, but considering they were heavily engaged in beating back Burmese invasions during this period, they were in no military position to do anything but acquiesce to this fait accompli. His later cession of what is called Province Wellesley in 1800 to the British further eroded Kedah-Thai relations.

By the first decade of the nineteenth century Siam was in a stronger military position than it had been for more than half a century and decided it was time to flex its muscles in the direction of what it considered its recalcitrant Malay vassals.

Pattani was the first to feel the Siamese wrath when it was attacked in 1791 after failing to supply its annual tribute to Bangkok. The sultan was killed in battle and some 4,000 Pattani's were brought to Bangkok as slaves, unintentionally spreading the Islamic faith at the same time.

A rebellion in 1808 was put down with force. After this revolt, Pattani was divided into seven districts and placed under the direct rule of the Raja of Ligor (modern-day Songkhla).

In 1809, the Sultan of Kedah was given orders to supply troops, vessels and rice to aid Siam in retaking the island of Phuket which had been occupied by the Burmese. There was irony is this action considering Kedah had previously claimed overlordship of the island in the mid-eighteenth century, when it was erroneously called Junk Ceylon.

In 1813, at the behest of the Siamese, an embassy from Kedah was sent to the court of the Sultan of Perak, urging the latter to pay tribute to Siam or face the consequences. Five years later, King Rama II ordered Sultan Ahmad Tajuddin Halim Shah of Kedah to attack Perak and force the latter to submit as a vassal of Siam.

Sultan Tajuddin did as he was instructed, but realised from the outset the Siamese aim was to weaken both Kedah and Perak prior to an invasion by the Siamese army and subsequent subjugation. The army of Kedah managed to subdue Perak after a campaign lasting more than a year. In 1819 the newly-installed ruler of Perak sent tribute to Bangkok, while at the same time a serious cholera epidemic afflicted Kedah.

The time looked right for King Rama II to launch a direct assault on Kedah, but an equally serious cholera outbreak occurred in Bangkok in 1820, eventually killing an estimated 20 percent of the city's inhabitants.

In 1821 the Siamese monarch invited Sultan Tajuddin to Bangkok to pay homage. The sultan, fearing assassination, refused to make the trip. This was the pretext required by Siam to launch an attack.

An army, under the command of the governor of Nakhon Sri Thammarat, marched overland to invade Kedah while a fleet anchored off the port of Alor Setar and troops sacked the town. It would lay abandoned for more than 20 years.

The fort at Kuala Kedah was overcome by treachery. It is claimed a Siamese fleet sailed into view on 12 November and the commander of the fort, one Bendahara Dato Paduka Maharaja Sura, being unsure of Thai intentions, welcomed them with some ceremony. He was giving the Siamese a guided tour of the fort when the Raja of Ligor, Phya Buri Sakmuton, suddenly ordered his men to attack. Despite this, they were unable to capture the sultan. It is claimed Sultan Tajuddin fled on elephant back, throwing coins along the way in an effort to delay his pursuers.

King Phra Phutthaloetla Naphalai, Rama II

He managed to make his way to Penang where he sought and received the protection of the British governor. Sultan Tajuddin hoped to persuade the British to come to his aid and restore his lost possessions. While there was sympathy for his cause on Penang, the East India Company government in India was convinced there was no long term benefit for them in becoming embroiled in conflicts on the Malay peninsula.

At the same time as the attack on Kedah took place, a Siamese army invaded Perak and succeeded in occupying the state. The occupation proved short-lived when the Sultan of Selangor attacked the Siamese occupiers and forced them out of Perak.

When the First Burmese War broke out in March 1824 the exiled Kedah sultan's fortunes turned for the worse. Siam was enlisted as an ally with the British, although Siamese troops took no part in the two-year conflict.

The 1826 Burney Treaty, which opened up trade relations between Britain and Siam further compromised the exiled ruler's position. The signing of the trade treaty led to a promise by the Siamese they would not pursue territorial aims beyond the northern Malay states they already claimed as vassals.

While the Kedah exiles on Penang were not given any hope of reclaiming their lands with British government help, there were plenty of local traders and businesspeople willing to covertly supply weapons and sailing vessels in exchange for gold and rice. The Kedah resistance movement would eventually grow strong enough for an attempt to be made to oust the Thai occupation forces.

The Jewel Robbery that Baffled the Best

It looked the perfect crime. When a box containing a string of 252 specially-made pearls and other valuable pieces of jewellery, ordered by Queen Saovabha Phongsri (the mother of the future King Vajiravudh, Rama VI), from a reputable agent in Britain and insured for £10,000, arrived in Bangkok in the middle of 1909, it was found to be empty. For almost three years the whereabouts of the pearls remained a mystery while police and diamond merchants followed a trail leading from Bangkok to Singapore, Penang, Australia, Batavia (now Jakarta), Colombo, Paris, and London.

Queen Saovabha Phongsri

When King Chulalongkorn made his second visit to Europe in 1907, among those accompanying him was Queen Saovabha Phongsri. In April 1909, Queen Saovabha arranged for a rope of pearls and other pieces of expensive jewellery to be been made up by the Association of Diamond Merchants, Jewellers, and Silversmiths Limited of Trafalgar Square in London.

After completing their commission, the jewellers carefully packed the items in a strong wooden box secured with four big red seals. According to some accounts, this box was placed aboard a German steamer bound for Bangkok and deposited in its strongroom. In other accounts the box was placed in the strongroom of a steamer bound for Hong Kong. When it arrived at that British colony the box was then taken to Bangkok. Either way, when the Court Chamberlain in Bangkok opened the box it was found to be empty, even though none of the four seals did not appear to have been broken. It was as if the jewels had simply vanished.

Although the pearls were insured, the insurance company refused to pay out until strenuous efforts had been made to recover the jewellery. Representatives of the Association of Diamond Merchants would spend literally thousands of pounds following up leads in the search for the pearls over the next year and a half before finally reaching a definite suspect. Their only hope at recovering the pearls and tracking the thief, or thieves, lay with the chance someone would eventually try and sell some of the distinctive pearls.

For almost 18 months the trail was cold and the jewellers association investigators completely baffled by the seemingly perfect crime. There were early suggestions that close inspection by experts revealed the seals on the strongbox were very cleverly executed copies of the originals. This meant the theft may well have occurred before the pearls even left Britain, but this idea was soon discarded when a second and more plausible explanation came to light.

The thief, or thieves, worked out it was not necessary to disturb the seals in order to get at the jewels. The lid of the strongbox was made in two pieces, tongued and grooved. One piece was 22.5 centimetres (nine inches) wide; the other was 15 centimetres (six inches) wide. By taking out the screws securing the 15cm piece, it was possible to slip it out of the larger piece. After cutting through the zinc lining on the box it was then a simple matter to remove the pearls and other items. After replacing the 22.5cm lid and refastening the screws there was no evidence of tampering. This knowledge simply expanded the number of possible scenarios for the theft: from inside Britain, on the steamer, or at its final destination in Bangkok and anywhere in-between.

The first clue came late in 1910 when it was learned that 33 pearls suspected as having belonged to the original rope had been sold to a dealer in Singapore. This dealer, a man of doubtful character, was traced to Paris in early 1911. When the investigators found him to ask questions, they made sure to keep their pistols within easy reach.

The dealer claimed he had already sold the pearls, but gave investigators the name of the man who sold the dealer the pearls. He was Paul de Boseck, a former wharfinger (owner), who had been working in Bangkok at the time the box containing the jewellery arrived. The box was in his possession for about five hours before being delivered to the Grand Palace.

Investigators soon learned de Boseck had sold a pair of the distinctive pearls to a bookmaker in Singapore. They travelled to Singapore and interviewed the bookmaker who told them he had already sold the two pearls to another bookmaker, who took them to Australia. This second bookmaker was found and the pearls brought back to Singapore where a director of the Association then purchased the pearls and positively identified them as having belonged to the original rope. He secured an arrest warrant for Paul de Boseck and the hunt was on.

The Association investigators traced de Boseck first to Batavia in the Dutch East Indies and then Ceylon, but lost his trail. That was in June 1911. In December a contact in the Straits Settlement (Singapore) government told investigators de Boseck was in England.

He was traced to an address in London and on 4 January 1912 Paul de Boseck was arrested by London police led by Detective Chief Inspector Bower.

Formally identified as Jules Paul de Boseck, alias Paul de Boseck (but also spelled Bosach and Debusick in some accounts), the alleged thief was a tall, slim 31-year-old (although other accounts stated he was 32) journalist. He had lived and worked in Bangkok as well as Singapore, but it would later be revealed he had led a something of a double life.

De Boseck was remanded under the Fugitive Offenders Act and charged with receiving jewellery which had been stolen at Bangkok. He submitted a written statement to the court noting he was known in Bangkok as lending money on goods and jewellery.

At his first hearing before a magistrate at the Bow Street courts in London, de Boseck was not represented by legal counsel. Inspector Bower, in the witness box, was asked by de Boseck, "Are you speaking of the two pearls I gave a bookmaker named Cohan or Cowan at Singapore in settlement of a debt?"

The police officer replied that he was, at which point de Boseck claimed he didn't know the pearls were stolen.

Bower replied, "It is alleged you gave a bookmaker at Singapore one or more of those stolen pearls. One of those pearls has been identified as a portion of some valuable jewellery which was handed to you when you were at Windsor's Wharf, at Bangkok, to forward to the Queen of Siam."

De Boseck countered by saying a large number of cases of jewellery went through his hands while he was in Bangkok. Bower then asked, "…do you wish to tell me whom you got them from?" The defendant said he needed to talk with his solicitor first.

De Boseck then attempted to regain the initiative by adding that when he lived at one of his three known addresses in England he went by the name of Charles Chilsworth. He claimed he adopted this name "when making enquiries respecting a political offence in Java [then part of the Dutch East Indies] and I retained it in all correspondence in connection with that case. I placed the result of my enquiries before the Chinese Minister at The Hague, and corresponded with him always in that name." The use of a pseudonym and reference to a clandestine inquiry reaching to the highest levels seemed intended to cast de Boseck in a Sherlock Holmes-style light.

He ended his defence by saying, "I parted with the pearls quite openly at Singapore, and had a receipt for them, but I think I destroyed it when I left Singapore with all other papers relating to my racing there. The receipt contained the weight and description of the pearls."

Despite his defence, de Boseck was committed to be extradited to the Straits Settlement for trial and left Britain in April 1912. Arriving in Singapore he duly went to court.

Between that first hearing in February 1912 in London and his trial in Singapore, De Boseck refined his story. He claimed a steamer's clerk who had lost heavily at gambling applied for a loan of 2,000 ticals, using a small box of pearls as security. De Boseck claimed he loaned the Chinese man just 920 ticals and received a receipt for 1,000 ticals. The following day the Chinese man told de Boseck he had lost all this money and asked him if he would buy the pearls. De Boseck claimed he asked the Chinese man where the pearls had come from, and he admitted they had been stolen, but did not say who the rightful owner was.

In his statement to the court de Boseck wrote, 'I understood [the pearls were] part of a cargo. I gave him another 500 ticals, and the pearls became mine by purchase. My object in not informing the police of the occurrence was threefold – (1) I feared the worry and annoyance the matter would cause me, as I was in a very bad state of health. I was suffering from facial paralysis and brain trouble, due to the climate, opium, and other causes; (2) it was only a little while back that I had made a continued attack in the press on the police and the rottenness of the system. This caused a radical change to be made, one of the Royal princes who was then in charge being transferred to another department; (3) it was a notorious matter that stolen property was dealt with with immunity, the native police usually retaining it, when seized, for their own private benefit, and rarely restoring it to the rightful owners.'

With what was essentially a very weak defence, it was no surprise de Boseck was found guilty at the end of May 1912 and sentenced to two years in prison for possession of stolen property. It was only with the conviction of de Boseck that the £10,000 insurance money was paid to the Association of Diamond Merchants, almost three years following the theft.

In the end, only the two pearls sold by de Boseck in Singapore were ever recovered from the original necklace of 252. The remaining 250 are now scattered all over the world.

Front Palace Crisis of 1874-1875

Just seven years after King Mongkut's (Rama IV) death of malaria in 1868, Siam and its monarchy were rocked by a crisis that came close to ending in civil war.

Chulalongkorn, Mongkut's eldest son and his legitimate heir and successor was just 15 years old and a regent, or Kalahom, was appointed by the Senabodi - the council of royal advisers - until he gained his majority. Since Chulalongkorn (King Rama V) had also contracted malaria at the same time as his late father and seemed unlikely to live, the regent, Suriyawongse, appointed Prince Wichaichan, the monarch's first cousin, as his heir-apparent and therefore second king or Uparat. If Chulalongkorn did die prematurely, then Prince Wichaichan would be in debt to Suriyawongse.

Prince Wichaichan

Chulalongkorn, although unwell, recovered sufficiently to be able to take control of his government, much to the chagrin of the regent. He was an intelligent young man and recognised the need for Siam to make reforms that would place it in a better position to resist the imperial aims of France and Britain. Nevertheless, his overall power base was fragile. His mother was dead and her relatives were, as the monarch later wrote to one of his sons, 'either unreliable or they were not in key government positions.' The relatives on his father's side he claimed were, 'under the power of the regent, and had to protect their own interests and their own lives, and most did not support me in any way.'

Chulalongkorn also realised those government officials who were loyal to him tended to be in minor positions and he could not hope for help from his brothers and sisters, all of whom were younger. His constant sickness, youth, lack of knowledge of government affairs and recognition that he was virtually alone might have caused a lesser man to succumb. King Rama V was to prove that he was a man of some mettle and as he approached his majority (his 20th birthday) he prepared to take up the reins of power.

From 1872 onwards, Chulalongkorn began to exercise increasing authority over his realm and instituted a series of radical reforms (including the sale of government-owned opium dens and gambling houses) designed to both increase the power of the monarchy while reducing the control of the lesser nobles and civil servants, as well as the regent.

In November 1873, Chulalongkorn was officially crowned as King Rama V and Suriyawongse relinquished the regency. The monarch created a Royal Privy Council and attempted to abolish slavery, paying money to slave owners as compensation. However, slavery was to continue until being outlawed in 1905.

In 1874 the new Privy Council, consisting of 56 appointees, announced they would nominate Chulalongkorn's eldest son (at the time just three years old) to succeed the king, thereby denying the possibility of the throne to Prince Wichaichan. This proposal was opposed by Suriyawongse and the supporters of the second king, all of whom saw their power base being eroded by Chulalongkorn's reforms.

Supposedly the Uparat, at the behest of his advisers, became determined to launch a coup and install himself as the sole ruler of Siam. On the night of 27 December 1874, he allegedly had the Grand Palace in Bangkok, Chulalongkorn's residence, set afire and then arrived on the scene with a force of armed men, ostensibly to help douse the flames. Chulalongkorn's guards refused Wichaichan's men entry to the burning palace and the fire was successfully doused without outside assistance.

However, the British Consul Thomas Knox and Newman, his deputy, in memorandums to the British Foreign Office, alleged that it was Chulalongkorn who was conspiring to remove the Uparat.

It is just possible the incident was a misunderstanding or was deliberately escalated by parties on both sides. When the fire was first noticed in the Grand Palace, the alarm was sounded and members of the Uparat's household prepared to go and assist in putting it out. However, the fire was quickly brought under control and it is possible someone then alleged the Uparat was preparing to send troops to attack the Grand Palace. From there the situation simply deteriorated.

At the beginning of January 1875, Prince Wichaichan sought asylum with the British Consulate, claiming he and his family and supporters were in fear of their lives. Siam looked to be hovering on the brink of civil war.

On 5 January, King Chulalongkorn sent a note to the Uparat: 'The present events are great and unprecedented and I am much grieved, why should Your Royal Highness have gone to stay with the British Consul? … I had no intention to kill Your Royal Highness... I am not angry with Your Royal Highness, but Your Royal Highness is angry with me and I am very sorry it should be so. By such events as these the reputation of this reign is imperiled for both of us. What further do you propose with a view to a reconciliation…If you have any proposal to make for good order and the end of doubt and restoration of happiness, write to me and tell me.'

Thomas Knox was on holiday in Europe when the crisis erupted. In a memorandum to the British Foreign Office dated 16 January 1875 he wrote Chulalongkorn was surrounded by what he termed '...a very bad set and he himself [Chulalongkorn] a mere puppet in their hands.'

The various foreign legations in Bangkok had requested naval support and within a week there were three warships, one each from France, Britain, and the United States lying in the Bangkok roadstead. According to one diplomat, '...The presence of these vessels, and the fact that the 2d King was in Asylum at the British Consulate, assured peace, and confidence was partially restored, but business languished: in fact, while negotiations have been going on, trade has been flat.'

In mid-February, Sir Andrew Clarke, the Governor of Singapore, arrived with two British warships while the following day, Admiral Ryder, the commander of British Naval Forces in the East Indies, arrived from Hong Kong. The British pair, with the added help of the American envoy in Bangkok, set about mediating the dispute between King Chulalongkorn and Prince Wichaichan and after a spending more than a month ensconced in the British legation, the Uparat returned safely to his palace.

Chulalongkorn managed to cling on to power, but realised his campaign of radical reforms would have to be put on hold until such time as he could gain control of the various arms of his government. Knox believed 'the whole affair was an intrigue on the part of the King to make himself despotic...'

The U.S. envoy was of the opinion that, 'The troubles were undoubtedly fomented in the first instance, by the Acting British Consul-General here, with a view to increase English influence...'

Whatever the truth of the incident, Chulalongkorn remained politically vulnerable and had to wait until 1888 before all the key positions within the government had been filled by his personal appointees. It was only then that he was able to re-embark on the series of reforms stifled in 1875. One of these was to eliminate the position of Uparat (who had died in 1884), thereby removing the potential for future conflict within the ruling Chakri dynasty. The dissolution of the office was dramatised by the simultaneous carving up of the Front Palace. A section was given over to the army, another substantial area became the site of the National Museum and a smaller portion was set aside to house the daughters of the last two Uparat's. Their sons were excluded, perhaps to forestall any suggestion of a hereditary right to the now defunct office.

Prajadhipok's visit to the United States

In 1931 King Prajadhipok (Rama VII), accompanied by Queen Bharni, met President Herbert Hoover, becoming the first reigning monarch of an Asian state to enter the White House.

As a *TIME* reporter noted, Rama VII was, 'the only monarch absolute both in theory and in fact...' Just over 14 months later the 'absolute' part of monarchical power would be swept away in a coup and within four years Prajadhipok would become the only one of the ruling Chakri dynasty to have abdicated.

King Prajadhipok, Rama VII TIME magazine 1931

In April 1931 though, he was treated with a measure of respect and diplomatic protocol from President Hoover and his cabinet, and with some bemusement and not a little patronising from the American press.

In fairness, *TIME* did make a number of positive statements regarding the military preparedness and economic position of Siam at the time: 'Today the Siamese Army is modern, mechanized. Siamese build all their own airplanes, importing only the motors. The Royal

Siamese Air Mail bi-weekly service has been maintained for seven years, 44,000,000 pounds of mail and merchandise have been carried, with two accidents, no deaths. Siamese are proud that 91% of their paper money is covered by securities readily convertible into gold, almost a world record. They are proud that their budget has balanced for years, grateful that King Prajadhipok has cut the royal civil list 30%, pepped up princely officials by discharging dullards no matter how royal they may be.'

Prajadhipok had come to the United States by steamer, first paying a visit to Emperor Hirohito in Japan. While the emperor conversed with his fellow ruler in Japanese, Prajadhipok replied in English. Naturally, an interpreter filled in the blanks.

After leaving Tokyo, the royal steamer sailed across the Pacific, eventually landing for the first time in North America at Vancouver in Canada. Here they boarded the Canadian-Pacific's private railway car Van Home, to which was attached another series of Pullman cars to accommodate the remainder of the royal entourage as well as security personnel.

In theory, King Prajadhipok was travelling incognito, passing himself off as the Prince of Sukhothai. According to the newspaper reports he would only officially become the King for a 48-hour period while in Washington.

The private train crossed into the United States at around midnight on 19 April 1931 at a place called Portal in North Dakota.

The chief reason for the trip, and hence one of the reasons for travelling incognito, was the monarch needed delicate cataract surgery on one eye. After fulfilling his official duties and being treated to a State dinner by President Hoover, Prajadhipok underwent surgery. It proved successful and he and Queen Bharni remained in the United States recuperating at the New York home of a wealthy widowed American lady.

The royal entourage returned to Bangkok in late October 1931. The *TIME* correspondent claimed the morning after his return King Prajadhipok was up early with plans to enact a new law to allow the citizens of Bangkok to elect their own municipal officers.

Kedah's War of Independence, 1831-1843

After being ousted by the Siamese in 1821 and fleeing to British-controlled Penang, Sultan Tajuddin of Kedah (Quedah as it was then spelt in newspapers) never gave up hope of one day returning in triumph to his homeland and evicting the Siamese occupiers.

There was a great deal of underground support for the Sultan but it took 10 years before a concerted effort was made to regain Kedah. The task fell to Sultan Tajuddin's son Tunku Ku Din. In 1831 he led a force of 3,000 Malays from Prai into Kedah and managed to catch the Siamese off guard. They recovered quickly and sent an army of 7,500 men accompanied, it is claimed, by 3,000 elephants (more likely 300) to retake Kedah.

Forced to retreat, Ku Din, and a few hundred of his followers, took refuge in Kuala Kedah fort. The Siamese were unable to breach the walls but, after building wooden siege towers to overlook the defences, they were able to pour musket fire inside the compound. Despite this the siege lasted three months before the Siamese were able to breach the defences. Ku Din was killed and his severed head sent to Bangkok.

Kedah remained a trouble spot and in 1838 yet another effort was made to shake off the Siamese yoke. Sherard Osborn, later an admiral and Arctic explorer, was serving with the British navy in Malayan waters at the time of the rebellion and later wrote an account of what he had seen. This was published in 1857 as *The Blockade of Kedah in 1838: A Midshipman's Exploits in Malayan Waters.*

Osborn noted the Malays had prepared their attack in secret, waiting to strike at the opportune moment. They had 2,000 men and more than 40 boats based at Batu Putih, near Acheh in Sumatra. They had received supplies of arms, ammunition and other materials smuggled to them by British and local merchants in Penang who were sympathetic to the Sultan of Kedah's cause.

Opportunity arose when British warships patrolling the Kedah coast in support of the Siamese occupation were diverted to Terengganu in July 1838 to engage Malay pirates. The Kedah Malays launched an attack across the unguarded straits, linked up with smaller fleets of Malays which had secretly gathered in the numerous mangrove-shrouded river estuaries along the Kedah coast and attacked the 80-man Siamese garrison holding the fort at Kuala Kedah. The Siamese were easily overcome with only one man killed on either side. According to a report in the Singapore Free Press published on 23 August, 'It appears…the [Siamese] in their retreat massacred about twenty Malay district chiefs of the territory…on a suspicion of having instigated or confederated with the invading force which had thus a second time wrested Quedah from their barbarous domination.'

British Admiral Sherard Osborn

The report went on to claim that Malays from within British-controlled Province Wellesley as well as surrounding areas were flocking into Kedah to join their brethren in ousting the Siamese occupiers.

Gathering further strength, the Malays drove the Siamese out of Kedah and then invaded southern Siam. They captured Perlis, Setul (Satun) and Trang, the latter described by the *Penang Gazette* as a place where *'great numbers of Quedah Malays were detained as captives by the [Siamese]'.* Osborn wrote that the Malay fleet at Trang consisted of more than 50 vessels, each bearing some light cannon and swivel guns.

The Kedah Malays then entered Pattani where four of the seven regions of that state had risen in revolt against the Siamese. At one point an estimated 300 Siamese troops who had been captured by the Malays were summarily executed, their bodies thrown into a reservoir. Such was the nature of warfare in the jungles of Southeast Asia. There was no doubt the Siamese would perform in an equally sanguine manner if the opportunity arose.

Swelled by reinforcements from Pattani to an estimated 10,000 men, the Malays took the war into Siam proper and laid siege to Singora (Songkhla). The defenders of Singora numbered some 2,000 Siamese and 500 Chinese troops. The Malays hoped to keep the Siamese on the defensive until the beginning of the monsoon, by which time they hoped Kedah would be better prepared to withstand a full-scale invasion.

The British came to the aid of their Siamese allies in December 1838 when HMS *Hyacinth* (18 guns) left Penang and anchored off Kuala Kedah, just out of range of cannon shot, in order to blockade the town and fort. Three gunboats, HMS *Pearl,* HMS *Emerald* and HMS *Diamond* patrolled the coast between Kuala Kedah and Palau Bunting aiming to disrupt any waterborne movement of troops and supplies.

At around the same time, a Siamese army estimated at 10,000 strong and accompanied by elephants invaded Kedah and cut off the Malay force besieging Singora. The besiegers were soon compelled to raise the siege and attempt to rejoin their comrades inside Kedah.

According to Osborn, a Siamese warship joined the British blockade at Kuala Kedah but anchored further away to avoid Malay cannon fire. The British invited the Siamese captain to come closer to the blockading line but he would shake his head and repeat 'Tidak bagus' ('No good'), according to Osborn. The British asked the Siamese commander a few more times if he would care to move closer but each time the refrain was the same. Not knowing the name of the Siamese warship, the British christened it the 'Tidak bagus'.

The blockade by the British appears to have been undertaken with little relish. A report in the *Penang Gazette* noted how HMS *Hyacinth* had spent eight days in port at Georgetown before returning to the blockade. The local press in Penang were clearly on the side of the local natives against the Siamese. In a brief report in the 23 June 1839 edition of the newspaper wrote about the blockade and ended with the line, *'which, bye the bye, we heartily wish had never been undertaken.'*

Gradually the Siamese army tightened its grip around Kuala Kedah, terrorizing the local villagers as they went. Many local inhabitants took to their boats in an attempt to escape the war, but the vessels were not sufficiently seaworthy to take people to places such as Penang or Prai. Instead, the boats anchored beneath the guns of the blockading British warships.

Osborn noted, *'We lay at anchor with a black mass of native vessels of every size and shape...Many of the canoes threatening to sink alongside, we were forced to take the unfortunates upon our decks, adding still more to the scene of confusion.'* Osborn claimed more than 3,000 people, mostly women, children and the elderly, were crammed into 120 or so boats of varying sizes and shapes.

The Siamese siege of Kuala Kedah fort was so intense the British warships moved further out to sea as cannon balls flew over the fort and were landing too close for comfort. Not a single shot was fired by the Malays at the British blockade. The town of Kuala Kedah was occupied by the Siamese and snipers attempted to pick off the less than 200 defenders of the fort. A sortie was launched into the town on the night of 19 March 1839, but the Malays were caught and cut to pieces. The fort fell the next morning.

Osborn wrote later, *'Nothing but a sense of duty could prevent one from sympathizing in the efforts made by these gallant sea-rovers to regain their own...Like spaniels, the natives of the whole sea-board of the Indian peninsula lick the hand that chastises them: not so the Orang Melayu; and we Englishmen should be the first to honour a race who will not basely submit to abuse or tyranny.'*

The war of independence was over, but in its place came a war of shrewd diplomacy. In 1842 Raja Zainal Rashid or Tengku Dai, the Sultan's eldest son, went to Bangkok to talk with King Rama III. It is suggested this move was at the instigation of the British. The timing might well have been right as the British were engaged in the First Opium War with China and King Rama III was making aggressive noises in the direction of Cochin China (Vietnam), threatening an invasion of what was a Chinese tributary state.

Tengku Dai offered to accept Siamese suzerainty if the throne of Kedah was restored to the Sultan. The King agreed, although the Sultan was forced to accept the permanent annexation of Setul and Perlis. So, in 1843, after 21 years of rebellion, Kedah was once more restored to the position of a Malay sultanate.

The fateful end to the HTMS *Prasae* during the Korean War

On 7 January 1951 the Thai corvette HTMS *Prasae* was caught in a blinding snowstorm just over 100 kilometres behind the front lines of her United Nations (UN) allies on the east coast of the Korean peninsula. In freezing conditions the *Prasae* was hurled onto the shoreline near the village of Yang-yang and became stranded, leading to a frantic attempt at salvaging her before the practically defenceless vessel could fall into North Korean hands.

HTMS Prasae beached in Korea

At this point UN forces were in retreat after an estimated 400,000 Chinese 'volunteers' joined the North Koreans in launching a counter-attack. In an effort to delay the advance, UN commanders ordered naval vessels to operate as far inshore as possible to provide inland bombardment, despite the dreadful weather conditions. These orders contributed to the grounding of the *Prasae,* one of four Thai warships sent to aid the UN war effort.

The *Prasae* had been commissioned in April 1943 as the British warship HMS *Betony,* serving until March 1945 when she was loaned to the Indian Navy and recommissioned as HMIS *Sind.* She returned to the British in May 1946 but in 1947 was sold to the Thai navy and renamed *Prasae.*

By the time supporting US naval units- including USS *Endicott, Bolster, Comstock* and *Manchester* began arriving- the *Prasae* had been subjected to severe damage from the pounding surf. Heavy swells washed away on-deck equipment. The first US helicopter at the scene, flown by a man named John Thornton, was unable to raise any other vessel by radio contact. He put down near the stranded ship and his radio officer made contact with the US liaison officer aboard the *Prasae* who instructed the helicopter to go out to the *Bolster* and bring in a salvage officer named Lieutenant Dudley. A landing craft from the *Bolster* had earlier attempted to reach *Prasae* but had been shattered by the seas and the crew drowned.

Thornton told the liaison officer North Korean troops were about one and a half kilometres away, entrenched behind a series of low-lying ridges. The biggest concern was how to keep the North Koreans away and salvage the *Prasae* in such treacherous weather conditions.

Trying to put Dudley aboard the stranded Thai warship in 30-knot winds proved impossible. Two attempts were made and the second ended in disaster. A sudden wave struck the ship, which bucked and the helicopter, operating with the barest minimum of space, was sucked into the superstructure and crashed. The disintegration of the helicopter caused explosions of onboard ammunition and led to fires aboard the corvette. Amazingly Dudley escaped with only broken ribs while Thornton and his crewman also survived.

Crewmen attempted to put out the fires with hoses, but water pressure was limited. Other sailors valiantly took anti-submarine depth charges aft to prevent them blowing up. Trapped sailors jumped overboard into the swirling and icy sea and struggled ashore, shivering in the sub-zero temperatures.

By the afternoon the fires dimmed and more rescue ships arrived. The *Comstock,* a Landing Ship Dock with heavy landing craft, sent a volunteer group of three crewmen, two doctors and a salvage officer who were fortunate to avoid being capsized as they reached the *Prasae.* They took off the injured, who were transferred to the beach to be taken off by helicopter.

Two Thais who jumped into the water were injured and in shock. They were to die later. Of the other 34 Thais and Americans on the beach, 18 needed to be airlifted away as quickly as possible.

Then the North Koreans began to move forward. Thai and US spotters on the *Prasae* relayed co-ordinates to the warships offshore who shelled the attackers. Despite heavy losses the North Korean kept advancing, knowing the fleet would have to cease fire soon or risk hitting their own men. A smart gunnery officer aboard a destroyer used his rapid-fire anti-aircraft guns at the lead North Korean elements, literally blowing them to pieces and forcing them to retreat. During the night the warships offshore kept firing bursts every 15 to 20 minutes.

On the second day the *Bolster* tried to move closer but the weather became even worse. A blizzard made visibility zero. *Prasae* had been hurled further up on the sand and the landing craft was also severely damaged and rendered unusable.

On the third day the boilers died and with it the heat. Fresh water ran out and supplies of everything were running low. The cold sapped the morale of the Thais.

The weather finally broke on the fourth day and for 14 hours attempts were made to drag the *Prasae* off the beach. The men were exhausted. That night the temperature dipped even further.

By 12 January, the fifth day, many Thai sailors were suffering pneumonia and there was no choice but to abandon ship. Detonating charges were placed, the crew stepped onto the snow and sand and flown out to the *Manchester*. After the charges went off *Prasae* was then raked with gunfire from the warships offshore.

In October 1951 the United States transferred two frigates, the USS *Glendale* and USS *Gallup* to the Thai navy, the latter being renamed HTMS *Prasae,* in honour of the vessel lost in the Korean conflict. The *Glendale* was renamed HTMS *Tachin.*

The *Gallup* had been launched in September 1943 and served in the Pacific around New Caledonia, New Guinea and the Philippines before being de-commissioned in August 1945. The *Gallup* was transferred under a lend lease agreement to the Soviet Union but returned to US control in 1949, laying at the Yokosuka naval yard in

Japan until brought back into service in October 1950 to serve in the Korean War.

This second HTMS *Prasae* was decommissioned in June 2000 and in December 2003 placed on public display as a memorial at the mouth of the Prasae River in Rayong province.

The British contribution to Thailand's war on Communism

On the morning of Thursday 17 June 1965, a band of the Scots Guards and the Argyll and Sutherland Highlander Regiment played at a unique ceremony in the district of Loeng Nok Tha in the province of Ubon Ratchathani. In what was one of the more incongruous sights to have ever been seen in the northeast of Thailand, an honour guard of Scots Guards, made up of troops then stationed in Malaysia, stood to attention as the guest of honour, Thai Prime Minister Thanom Kittikachorn, took the salute.

Thanom Kittikachorn was not a frequent visitor to the impoverished and generally much-neglected northeast, but this occasion was too important for him to miss. It involved the official opening and handing over of an airfield that had been constructed by a squadron of British army engineers, with help from the odd detachment of their Australian and New Zealand compatriots as well as other British corps.

The British involvement in the exercise could be traced back to the creation of the South East Asian Treaty Organisation (SEATO), a regional defence pact signed in Manila in September 1954 between the United States, Britain, France, Australia, New Zealand, Pakistan, Thailand, and the Philippines. All eight countries pledged to guarantee the security of the region, but specifically the sovereignty of South Vietnam, Laos, and Cambodia. SEATO was specifically designed to thwart the southward spread of communism.

With the coming to power of Mao Zedong and the Communist Party in China in 1949, the United States and its allies became increasingly embroiled in the internal politics of the countries to China's south. By the time the French were evicted from northern Vietnam, Laos and Cambodia in the mid-1950s, it appeared as though US president Dwight Eisenhower's 'domino theory' concerning the southward spread of communism might indeed threaten the independence of countries like Thailand, Burma, and Malaysia.

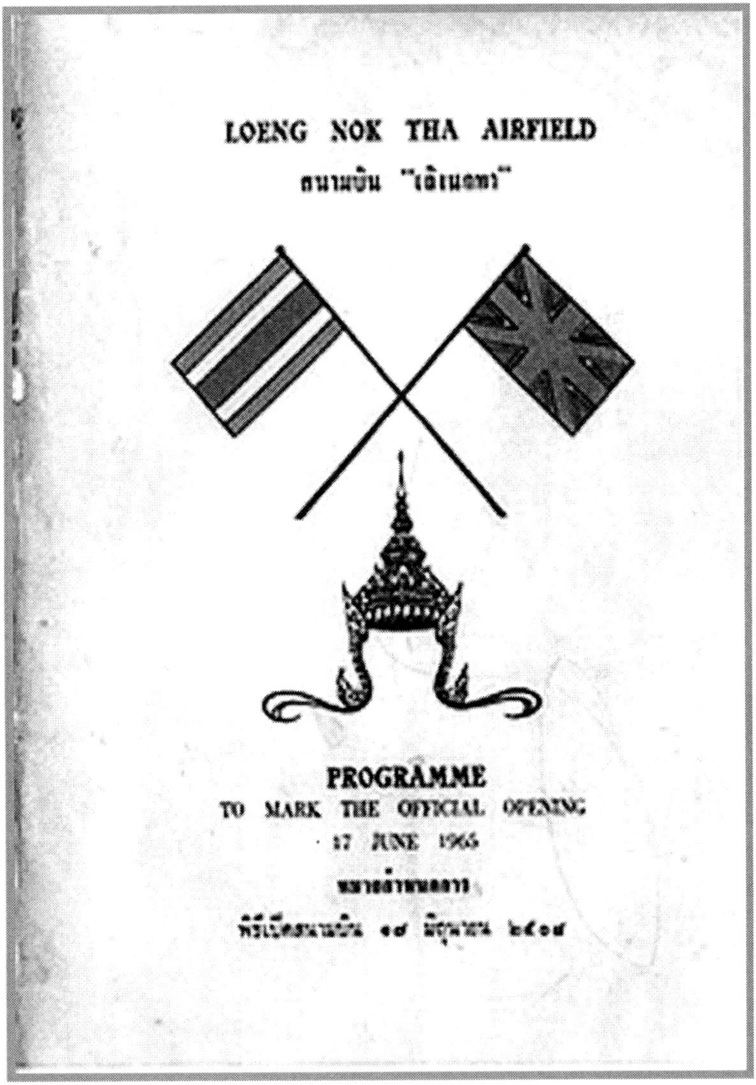

1965 17 June Official program

For the United States, Thailand's pivotal geographical position made it a prize that needed to be retained as a bulwark against the Chinese. Yet by 1950 there were nearly three million Chinese immigrants in Thailand, almost 16 percent of the total population of 18 million.

An estimated 40,000-60,000 Vietnamese refugees, most of whom had crossed into Thailand during the First Indochina War (1945-1954), settled predominantly in the northeast. Both the Chinese and Vietnamese immigrants and refugees were, in many cases, suspected of divided loyalties and by the end of the 1950s a burgeoning communist insurgency had begun, centred primarily in the northeast.

Naturally, suspicion fell on the Chinese and Vietnamese, many of the latter allegedly supporters of the North Vietnamese president Ho Chi Minh. A long article on Thailand published in *TIME* magazine in May 1966 wrote of the Vietnamese, '…with their own cadres, schools and tight internal organizations, and their distinctive ground-hugging houses, unlike those on stilts of the Thais, [they] are a built-in springboard for future trouble. But thus far the insurgency leadership is essentially Thai…'

In early 1963 the Americans, using the terms of the SEATO alliance, asked the British to supply engineers to help build an airfield, and later to aid in the construction of modern roads into the northeast. The British agreed, but insisted their men be unarmed so they would not attract the attention of communist insurgents operating in the region.

The British construction project was given the royal-sounding codename Operation Crown and was typical of the 'joint-nation aid programmes…launched in a bid to prevent this part of Thailand becoming another Vietnam.' The first units began arriving in January 1964.

Part of the money to build the airfield and roads came out of a 28 billion baht fund allocated to what was known as the First Development Plan, a five-year project begun in 1961.

A March 1967 article published in the *London Illustrated News* noted the engineers were part of the 'battle to stamp out Communism…a war that is being waged with tractors and bulldozers and a programme to rid the area of the isolation and poverty which give Communist propaganda its best chance.'

The all-weather tarmac airstrip, approximately 1,800 metres long, had to be carved out of the scrubland from scratch. When officers and men arrived in Loeng Nok Tha they spent the first three months building huts, water facilities, and installing electricity generators before serious work could begin on construction of the runway. From September until May the area is parched and dry, while the monsoon begins in June and the rain and resultant mud made work almost impossible. Yet the engineers installed storm-water drains in that first year which proved very effective at dispersing any floodwaters.

The first runway -the one officially opened that day in June 1965 by Thanom Kittikachorn - was made of tarmac. Even before it was ready for use it had begun to crack. George Trainor, who came to work on the airfield after it was opened, claimed, '…during construction underground water channels were compacted and blocked so that when the monsoons came the water got trapped under the strip and as it could not escape through these channels it came up under the tarmac causing it to lift and crumble.'

Malcolm Thomas, one of the first engineers assigned to the project, said the first plane to land on the tarmac was a three-seater light aircraft, flown by an American, 'for the sole purpose of taking Lieutenant-Colonel Orrell [the British commander] to see the runway from the air…' The second aircraft to come in was a British air force Canberra bomber.

After the official opening, during which an estimated three centimetres of monsoonal rain fell in less than quarter of an hour, work continued on the airfield, replacing the tarmac with a more solid concrete base. This took almost two years and when it was completed yet another official opening ceremony too place, although, as Trainor notes, 'as far as I remember the original 1965 plaque was never replaced.'

After June 1965, some 300 officers and men were set to work on constructing a 32-kilometre long road leading from the airfield and stretching into the province of Roi Et.

This road would eventually link up with another being constructed by Thai engineers, under American supervision. Five teak bridges were thrown across streams and rivers, with laterite, a brick-coloured rock quarried from the region used as the main ingredient for the tarmac. The British soldiers brought in topsoil to replace the laterite, thereby providing new rice paddies for villagers. The British engineers also sank a number of new wells 'in many villages where the people…formerly had to rely on bore water during the dry season.'

The *Illustrated News* article claimed the road was 'being built in a Communist-infested area, where the lack of communication has long left the villages and hamlets at the mercy of a terrorist movement directed by about 100 hard-core guerrillas. Village headmen, teachers, police and government officials have been attacked or killed. It is estimated that 40 percent of the people in the district are Communist sympathisers.' A nearby village, Ban Dan, located 13 kilometres from the main British camp had been quarantined by Thai troops and police because it was considered completely Communist.

Although the *London Illustrated News* article claimed there were only 100 hard-core guerrillas, stories in other publications referred to much higher numbers, whether for propaganda purposes or simple misunderstanding is hard to gauge.

During all the time the British operated in the region, the guerrillas never subjected them to an attack. Lieutenant-Colonel H. Browne, the commander of the British road-builders, attributed this to his squadron's strictly non-military role. "We have absolutely no military motive here whatsoever, and we could just as well be building a road in another province where there are no terrorists," he was quoted as saying. "But I suppose you could say that by building this road and providing communication between the villages and hamlets we are giving the area a means of developing itself, and in the long run helping defeat a Communist takeover of the district."

The British engineers spent four years in the northeast, finally departing in mid-1968. Unfortunately, their legacy was mixed. On a positive note, the airfield and road construction definitely improved communications over a wide area. On the negative side, despite the British and American efforts at winning hearts and minds, the communist insurgency escalated. Indeed, even as the Loeng Nok Tha airfield was being readied for handover in 1965, the Chinese foreign minister Chen Yi was predicting the northeast would soon erupt in revolt against the government in Bangkok. Certainly the numbers of insurgents grew.

When Thailand agreed to send troops to fight in South Vietnam in 1968, Thanom Kittikachorn was quoted by *TIME* magazine as saying, "Even today the Communists are infiltrating Thailand and increasing their subversive actions against our country." The magazine claimed there were 'at least 2,000 guerrillas' roaming the northeast.

An article published in a 1970 edition of the *Bangkok World* magazine claimed, 'Results from the "development stops Communism" policy have been poor, and the present situation strongly suggests we may have overlooked the real issues. It has been made sufficiently clear now that we cannot buy loyalty with wells or roads, and that being richer is no guarantee against insurgency...' The fundamental underlying problem, according to analysts, was the arbitrary and unfair distribution of wealth and power, with the politicians and military based in Bangkok viewed more as enemies of the people rather than as a benevolent government.

There were rumours the airfield at Loeng Nok Tha was used by the Central Intelligence Agency's (CIA) airline Air America for its clandestine incursions during the secret war against Laos, but this has never been confirmed. The remains of the airfield are still there, while the British-built road became part of a vast network that connected the northeast with the main national road system, thereby helping develop the region and playing a small but significant role in attempting to help the central government fight its war on communism in the region.

Anglo-Siamese agreement on Kelantan 1900-1902

For most of the nineteenth century the northern Malay states of Kelantan, Kedah, Perlis and Terengganu were autonomous territories owing allegiance to Siam and its monarch.

Palace of the Sultan of Kelantan, 1912

As Britain expanded its empire in the Asian and Southeast Asian region in the nineteenth century, successive governments, acting on the advice of the Foreign Office, held a general policy of seeing Siam remain independent. That said, the Colonial and India Offices were more concerned with improving local economic positions favourable to Britain and, while not overtly looking to dismember Siam, supported the government of the Straits Settlements (Singapore) in its desire to expand British influence over the southernmost of Siam's tributary states, especially Terengganu and Kelantan. The push towards 'extracting' these two states from Siam began as early as 1883.

One of the leading supporters of the belief Siam could be persuaded to part with territory on the Malay peninsula was George Curzon, who became parliamentary under-secretary of state for foreign affairs in 1895. With the Paknam crisis still fresh in the memory of Siam, Curzon felt they could be persuaded to relinquish control of Terengganu and Kelantan in gratitude for Britain's efforts at resisting the French in their planned occupation of the country.

Following the signing of the London Declaration in January 1896 between Britain and France, delineating the area of Siam that would henceforth be declared as a neutral zone and subject to the protection of both major powers, the British became concerned at the possibility of German expansion into the Malay peninsula. The Colonial Office were worried the Germans would attempt to establish a station between Tennasserim and northern Malaya as a kind of 'counterpart to Walfisch [Walvis] Bay in the middle of the German protectorate in Southwest Africa [now Namibia]'.

To circumvent this possibility, the Secret Convention of 6 April 1897 was signed between Britain and Siam, by which the latter agreed to exclude foreigners from gaining concessions in the west of the country. Strangely, Siam failed to gain corresponding assurances as to their sovereignty over the southern Malay states.

In 1899, Sultan Mansur of Kelantan died and was succeeded by Tengku Long Senik, later to be known as Sultan Muhammad IV. Certain members of the ruling classes in Kelantan did not support Sultan Muhammad and his position was only secured after Siamese troops were sent to the capital, Kota Bharu, to enforce the succession.

On 25 May 1900, King Chulalongkorn came to Kota Bharu to visit the new sultan. The King wanted to personally assess the political stability of Kelantan. A meeting took place aboard Chulalongkorn's ship with Sultan Muhammad and four other Kelantan leaders.

Chulalongkorn was satisfied with the early performance of Sultan Muhammad, but the latter's decision that same year to lease out almost one-third of his state (4,800 square kilometres) to the Duff Development Company was to prove the catalyst which would eventually see hegemony of Kelantan pass from Siam to Britain. The lease between Kelantan and the Duff Development Company, which had originally been engaged in dredging the streams running off the Kelantan River for gold, was signed on 10 October 1900.

The British government viewed the lease agreement in a different light to Siam, claiming the Siamese had no right to sanction its issue as they considered Kelantan an independent state.

At the height of the confrontation between Siam and Britain, Sultan Muhammad fled Kota Bharu by steamship and, after a brief sojourn in Singapore, arrived in Bangkok, where he stayed for two months.

The issue was resolved amicably between Britain and Siam with the signing of a joint declaration, known as the Anglo-Siamese Treaty, in London on 6 October 1902.

By the terms of the treaty, the British recognised Siam's suzerainty over Kelantan, Kedah, Perlis and Terengganu but stipulated these provinces would henceforth be administered by what was known as a Resident, a British adviser appointed by joint agreement between the Siamese and British governments.

On 25 July 1903 William Graham, an officer in the Indian Civil Service, and H.W. Thomson, an officer in the Federated Malay States Civil Service, accompanied by a police contingent, arrived in Kelantan from Bangkok aboard a Siamese naval vessel to take up their positions as Resident and Assistant Resident.

They remained at their posts until 3 March 1909, when Siam signed an agreement in Bangkok ceding Kelantan, Kedah, Perlis and Terengganu to Britain, partly because of an offer of a cheap railway loan by Britain. The agreement was ratified in July.

Tarutao: island of prisoners and pirates

In 1937 the government decided to construct a prison on the island of Tarutao, one of a group of islands in the Andaman Sea administered by the southern province of Satun.

A 30-metre-high (98 ft) limestone cliff near the old prison site.
Credit Argenberg - www.flickr.com/photos/argenberg/838870057/, CC BY 2.0

Tarutao was selected because it was hundreds of kilometres from Bangkok, remote, virtually uninhabited and, during the monsoon season from May to October each year, difficult to reach by boat. Basically, it would serve the same purpose for Siam that Devil's Island and Alcatraz served for France and the United States respectively.

Most of the island is covered by rain forest and, back in the 1930s and 1940s, crocodiles were plentiful. These were eventually hunted almost to extinction in the area.

The first operatives from the Department of Corrections arrived on Tarutao on 13 July 1938. The group was led by Luang Pitan Tantatai and consisted of 10 staff and guards and a number of prisoners.

They established a base at Talo Udang Bay, built an office and then constructed an 11-kilometre road to Talo Wao Bay and established a second office on that site. That road wasn't completed until June 1941.

The offices in Talo Udang Bay became the headquarters of the warden and in June 1941 the first group of 500 prisoners arrived. A second group of 500 came in September that same year.

The inmates came by train from Bangkok to Songkhla, then by truck across a dirt road to Koh Nok Pier just outside Satun where they were taken by motorboat to Tarutao. On other occasions, prisoners went by train from Bangkok to Kantang Pier in the province of Trang before being loaded onto a motorboat for the trip to the island.

A group of 80 political prisoners, many of them former government officials and military officers highly placed within the government prior to the overthrow of the absolute monarchy in 1932 were sent to Tarutao in 1941. Most had been involved in the failed Boworadet coup of October 1933. The government didn't want them to mix with the general prison population, so they were housed at a special area close to the beach at Talo Udang Bay.

One of the political prisoners was So Sethaputra, who had begun compiling a Thai-English/English-Thai dictionary whilst inside Bang Kwang prison in Bangkok. He had won a King's scholarship to study overseas and after returning to Siam worked for the civil service and contributed articles to newspapers. Some of his pieces were deemed too critical of the government and he was charged with sedition in 1934. The 30-year-old scholar managed to have reference books, stationery, and dictionaries smuggled into the prison so he could work on creating his Dictionary.

After So and his cellmates were caught with a radio they had smuggled into their cell they were sent to Tarutao. So continued to work on the Dictionary and completed the 4,000-page work during the Second World War, after being transferred to Surat Thani. His dictionary is still used today.

Five of the political prisoners escaped by paying money to four men who took them by boat to the safety of the Malay island of Langkawi, five kilometres to the south.

In 1943, Tarutao was declared the property of the Department of

Corrections, meaning all non-inmates or staff who lived on the island were forced to move elsewhere.

During its time as a prison it is estimated around 10,000 inmates were sent to the island with approximately 3,000 being housed at any one time. The largest concentration of prisoners was at Talo Wao Bay, housing around 2,000 men. Another 600 or so were accommodated at Talo Udang Bay with a further 200 located at Kramad Canal. Many hundreds died of malaria.

Due to water and food shortages brought about by the worsening military situation in the latter stages of the Second World War, the guards and prisoners on Tarutao were forced to go begging for food and other supplies from ships passing by the island. As the quantities of supplies given by some passing trading vessels proved insufficient for their needs, some people turned to piracy.

The action of the pirates continued after the surrender of Japan and was aided by the power vacuum that existed in the few months it took for the British to regain effective administrative control of the Malay States.

When the pirates began hijacking vessels travelling to Langkawi, the British asked the Thai government to clamp down. When the Thais proved unable to do so, the British government requested permission to undertake a punitive expedition against the pirates.

The request was granted and on 15 March 1946 a small Royal Navy force consisting of two vessels and 300 troops under the command of General Terray landed at Talo Wao Bay on Tarutao and began operations against the pirates. They destroyed the pirate bases, killed a number of the buccaneers and departed eight days later.

In 1949, the Department of Corrections closed down the Tarutao prison and it became vacant land. It was transferred to the control of the Forestry Department in 1974 and in April 1975 Tarutao became the first marine national park in Thailand.

A Foreign Journalists' view of Siam in the Decade of Militarism

By the middle of the turbulent decade of the 1930s, it was increasingly clear to Asia watchers that Japanese militarism, apart from its expansionist actions against China, was also eyeing the lucrative markets of Southeast Asia, and Siam was a premier prize in the region.

A young American journalist named Gareth Jones visited Siam in 1935 to determine if the rumours of Japanese domination of Siam, circulating from such diverse places as the Dutch East Indies (now Indonesia), British-controlled Singapore and Japan itself, were true.

In 1932, Japan had effectively annexed Manchuria from China, renaming it Manchukuo, placing a puppet emperor on the throne and declaring it a protectorate. Siam was the only country in the League of Nations that refrained from voting against the condemnation of Japan's conquest.

Jones' first despatch from Bangkok appeared in April 1935. He wrote: '…I was told in Java, [the Japanese] are pushing their Empire ever further Southwards and Westwards. They want to have a stronghold in Siam. They want to build a canal which would compare with the Panama Canal and which would enable them to dominate the markets of India and the power of the British in Asia. This Canal would be the Kra Canal and would make Singapore into a bigger "white elephant" than any owned by the Kings of Bangkok. They want to be masters of the route from Asia to India and to Africa.'

The American journalist stated, 'There is certainly a growing friendship between Siam and Japan…a leading Japanese authority said to me: "We Siamese regard Japan as an elder brother… an example to Siam of a country which has freed itself from Western influences and which has progressed rapidly. The young people here look up to the Japanese and say: 'If only we could do what they do'." One reason for increasing Japanese influence at the expense of the West was laid at the feet of returned Siamese soldiers who had fought in France during World War One. '…they returned with the tale of a bloody impoverished white race with its members at each others' throats.' It made the Siamese realise they were as good as their white counterparts and, 'The result is that many European advisers have left the country. That the Siamese State railways, which formerly had many British experts and foremen has today only one British worker and that Japanese experts are coming to take the place of whites. Recently cotton experts came from Japan and there are two Japanese officers of high rank in the Siamese Army…Many Siamese students now go to Japan. Recently a number of Siamese naval cadets, abandoning the tradition that the British Navy shall teach the future admirals of Siam, went to receive their training in the Japanese fleet...'

1941 anti-colonial cartoons

Japanese influence in the media was strong because local newspapers received most of their news via Rengo, the official Japanese news agency. Increasing trade ties also influenced the Siamese. In 1934, Japanese automaker Datsun sold a single vehicle in Siam. The next year the company opened a showroom in Bangkok to sell Japanese cars. By that time, Japanese manufacturers were already dominant in the radio accessories, silk, paper, bicycle, cement, and rubber goods markets.

In 1935, for the first time, a contract to construct railway bridges was given to Japan, even though there were 11 American and European firms also in the bidding.

Gareth Jones believed the answer to the question as to whether Japan was dominating Siam was in the negative. He claimed Siam was riding the wave of nationalism then sweeping the world and they were not willing to '...bow down before any nation...They are afraid of being dominated by the Japanese and they are too wise to place their fate in the hands of Nippon, when they have the French on one side of them and the British on the other.'

The vast numbers of Chinese immigrants in Siam made up the backbone of business in the country and they hated 'the Japanese and would fight any policy of placing Siam beneath Japanese protection.' Jones commented that when Japan invaded Manchuria, some Chinese servant boys in Bangkok smashed all Japanese-made crockery in the homes of their employers while storekeepers refused to buy or sell Japanese goods.

Jones made the point that 'British advisers still quietly control the finances of Siam and the Siamese money, which has the comic name of "ticul" (about 50c) is linked with sterling. "Does Japan dominate Siam?" I asked a leading English-man in Bangkok. He laughed quietly: "Have you any Siamese money?" he asked. I drew out a five-ticul note (about 2 dollars 50 c). "Read what is printed at the foot of the note," he commanded. I read, "Thomas de la Rue and Co., London". With calm confidence he said: "As long as the word 'London' stands on that Siamese bill, it is not Japan but another little island which will have the larger say in the Kingdom of Siam."'

He also claimed the prospect of the Kra Canal being constructed by the Japanese as '...one of the biggest myths of the century...For the Japanese to build a canal in Siamese territory across the Isthmus of Kra would cost a vast amount of capital. London would never lend the money for an anti-British scheme. Wall Street would not be so foolish as to put its finger in the pie. Tokyo is too impoverished to finance the Canal. Even if by some financial miracle the money were forthcoming, the Canal would be a failure, because no vessel would pay vast dues to save only two day's voyage and many ships round South Africa in order to save the dues on the Suez Canal. Nor would captains avoid such a rich free-trade port as Singapore, where they can pick up valuable freight. No, Singapore can rest calm as a symbol that Britain dominates the North from the Pacific to India.'

The revolution that had removed the absolute monarchy in 1932 '...had led to a military dictatorship and that the Army was the real master of Siam...' He reported soldiers were being sent to schools to demonstrate the use of military weaponry and asked the Education Minister why. "We believe in military drill and military training for the youth of Siam, because they give discipline and build character," the Minister is said to have replied.

'Throughout the East the rulers are watching Stalin, Hitler, Mussolini and Roosevelt and they are trying to make the State all-powerful. They wish to build factories and dig mines controlled by the State. They are battling against private enterprise and are creating all-mighty Government machines to dominate economic life. They are saying good-bye to the Nineteenth Century era of capitalism and opening the doors to State control, just as President Roosevelt is putting business under the watchful eye of the Government. The countries of Asia are working out their New Deal. The ideas of Hitler varied with the ideas of Stalin are finding a fertile soil in the countries of Asia. A fiery nationalism is wedded with Socialistic ideas. Militarism rampant marches side by side with hatred of capitalism.'

Jones finished his series with the following statement: 'The Siamese want with the help of the State to push forward the building of industry. Just as every nation in Asia now wants to buy less from America and Europe and produce all themselves, the Siamese want to see smoke stacks and factory walls rearing proudly above the shacks of Bangkok.' Half a century later, that scene was a reality in the Thai capital.

Sadly, Gareth Jones was killed by bandits in northern China in late 1935. He was just 30 years old.

First among Equals: Phrya Manoprakorn, Siam's First Prime Minister

The coup of 24 June 1932 launched by a group of civil servants and military officers who called themselves the Promoters, led to the replacement of the absolute monarchy for a constitutional framework under King Prajadhipok (Rama VII).

The Promoters created a political entity known as the People's Party and aimed to provide Siam with an ostensibly democratic form of government, modelled along the lines of the Westminster system in Britain, to fill the power vacuum.

A provisional constitution, drawn up Pridi Banomyong, a law professor and leader of the civilian section of the Promoters, was put into effect three days after the coup. On the same day all ministers, department heads and secretaries of the former monarchical government were compelled to resign.

King Prajadhipok reluctantly accepted the loss of his political power, accepting that the prestige of the monarchy was unimpaired. The Executive Committee of the People's Party became the provisional government and the Promoters asked the respected Phrya Manoprakorn Nithithada, a 47-year-old Judge of the Court of Appeals, to take the position of Chairman.

Phrya Manoprakorn Nithithada, better known simply as Phrya Mano, was born in Bangkok on 15 July 1884. He attended the prestigious Suan Kularb Vidhayalai school before winning a scholarship and going on to Assumption College and thence to England where he studied law.

Phrya Mano returned to Siam and worked in the Ministry of Justice and, in 1918, the barrister was appointed an adviser to King Prajadhipok. He was later appointed to the Court of Appeals as a Judge, a position from which he garnered great respect.

When Rama VII signed the temporary constitution on 27 June 1932, thereby ending the era of the absolute monarch, Phrya Mano was appointed Chairman of the People's Party, effectively making him the first Prime Minister of Siam.

From the beginning, Phrya Mano's position was tenuous, given that he was charged with leading a shaky coalition consisting of the various factions that had now taken control of the country.

Phraya Manoprakorn Nititada, 1st Prime Minister of Siam

He walked a fine line between the competing aims of Pridi Banomyong, the ambitious leader of the civilian faction of the People's Party, Colonel (later General and then Field Marshal) Pibul Songgram, the young and equally ambitious leader of the military wing and Colonel Phrya Phahon Polphayuhasena, better known as Phrya Phahon, the senior military member of the People's Party.

Nearly six months after the June coup, King Rama VII signed into being a permanent constitution and on 10 December Phrya Mano was confirmed as the nation's first Prime Minister. The King also issued a Royal Pardon to all the participants of the June revolution.

The new constitution allowed for the creation of a unicameral legislature to be known as the National Assembly. Half of the members were to be appointed by the government and the other half to be elected on a limited suffrage. It was planned that the entire

National Assembly would be elected after a period of 10 years or when half of the electorate had received a minimum of four years schooling, whichever came first.

The National Assembly, through the Cabinet, took control of the budget and could override a royal veto. Real power resided with the likes of Pridi Banomyong, Pibul Songgram and Phrya Phahon with Prime Minister Phrya Mano more a figurehead than a genuine leader. On 1 March 1933, with the country, like the rest of the world, in the grip of the Great Economic Depression, the Finance Minister Pridi Banomyong presented a National Economic Policy for the consideration of the National Assembly.

The policy, among other elements, called for the nationalisation of natural resources, and touched off a crisis within the ruling elite with his military rivals Pibul Songgram and Phrya Phahon accusing Pridi of being a communist.

Apart from Pibul Songgram and Phrya Phahon, Pridi's plan was completely unacceptable to the Prime Minister and in response Phrya Mano sought and received the permission of King Rama VII to suspend the current session of the National Assembly and rule by decree. This action took place on 1 April and, as Pridi's support base was centred on the National Assembly, he resigned from the People's Party and went into exile.

Emboldened by this political success, which turned him into a virtual dictator, Phrya Mano began to overreach himself. One of his first acts was to declare adherence to communism illegal and punishable by a prison term of 10 years.

Believing that his position of Prime Minister gave him a genuine mandate to control the direction of the country, Phrya Mano let it be known that he planned to shackle the military by denying them direct command of troops. It was clear he intended to wrest control of the military and pass it into civilian hands, specifically his own.

This proved too much for the military and army officers opposed to the civilian Prime Minister staged a successful and bloodless coup on 20 June 1933. Colonel Phrya Phahon was appointed Prime Minister and quickly restored the National Assembly.

Phrya Mano, who had been at a decidedly difficult helm for less than 12 months, left Bangkok and decided to go into exile in Malaya, settling in Penang where he was a neighbour of Prince Damrong Rajanubhab, who had left Siam after the 1932 coup.

Siam's first Prime Minister died in Penang on 1 October 1948, aged 64. In Penang there is, apparently, a street called 'Mano Road' named after the former leader.

Prince Mahidol of Songkhla, The Father of Modern Thai Medicine

The son of King Chulalongkorn (Rama V) and Queen Savang Vadhana, Prince Mahidol Adulyadej was born on 1 January 1892. At 13, he was ordained, like his brothers, as a Buddhist novice at Bovornnivet Temple and received the title of Prince of Songkhla.

He was sent to England and completed his formal education at the prestigious Harrow school.

HRH Prince Mahidol Adulyadej, Prince of Songkla

His father and the German monarch Kaiser Wilhelm II had struck up a friendship during a visit by the Thai ruler to Germany in 1897, and it was the wish of King Chulalongkorn that Prince Mahidol should continue his education by going to the Royal Prussian Military Preparatory College in Potsdam.

Apart from the military aspect of the college, there were also courses available in humanities and science, and Prince Mahidol took these up with enthusiasm, completing the Preparatory College at the age of 18.

Always physically frail, the Prince suffered from problems with his back, but these were cured at Potsdam. His physical ailments were more than likely the catalysts that led to Prince Mahidol's future intense interest in health and medicine.

The strict rules and regulations at Potsdam apparently suited the young Prince. He told a Thai colleague the discipline was, "... good. I like to be treated strictly. I was too comfortable in Siam, with everyone giving me everything."

After Potsdam, he spent two years at the Imperial Military Academy in Berlin, graduating in 1912. He entered the German Naval Academy at Flensburg, and at the same time was commissioned as a lieutenant in the Royal Thai Navy by his elder brother King Vajiravudh (Rama VI).

Prince Mahidol's formal military education ended in 1914, but with the outbreak of the First World War he was instructed by King Vajiravudh to return to (then) neutral Siam.

It was while serving in the Thai Navy that Prince Mahidol was invited on a canal tour by the Chief of the Royal Medical College, Prince Chainart-narenthorn. They stopped at a nearby hospital and went for a stroll. Prince Mahidol saw people sitting and lying on the ground underneath the trees in the compound and was told they were patients for whom no rooms were available.

Inside the hospital, the Prince later stated the rooms looked more like unkempt stables and became acutely aware that the standard of public health and of medical practitioners was seriously deficient in Siam.

This tour proved to be a turning point in Prince Mahidol's life. He expressed a desire to gain the necessary medical knowledge so he could help the sick and injured, and made application to his brother the King asking permission to terminate his naval career.

The King acquiesced and Prince Mahidol enrolled at Harvard University in the United States in 1916 to study public health and medicine. His first choice had been Edinburgh University in

Scotland, but the effect of the weather on his poor health meant Harvard was a better option.

His correspondence from that time shows a man who had clearly found his vocation in life. He stayed at a house in Boston, Massachusetts, registering simply as Mr. Mahidol Songkhla and one of his professors wrote he was a student who did "...not let details pass by."

To commence the task of building a core of well-educated and reliable medical staff, Prince Mahidol asked Prince Chainart-narenthorn to send four students to the United States on a scholarship with funds supplied by himself and his mother Queen Savang Vadhana.

One of the students happened to be 18-year-old Sangwan Talabhat, who was going to study nursing at Simmons College. Prince Mahidol met the four students at the train station and was soon courting Sangwan Talabhat. The pair married in Bangkok on 10 September 1920.

In 1921, Prince Mahidol received his Certificate of Public Health from Harvard and travelled on a holiday to Europe. Soon after, the Rockefeller Foundation made an offer to provide finance to assist in the development of medical and nursing education in Siam.

A senior official of the Foundation met with a former Thai Education Minister to prepare the groundwork for assistance. Further discussions took place between Prince Mahidol and senior Rockefeller Foundation officials with the Prince selecting suitable students to receive Foundation scholarships.

In 1923, Princess Galyani Vadhana, their first child and only daughter, was born in London, England.

Two months after the birth of their daughter, the family returned to Siam and in October the Prince was appointed Director-General of the University Department at the Ministry of Education. Medical assistance was provided by funds from the Rockefeller Foundation.

Prince Mahidol worked energetically at developing a new curriculum, acquired modern equipment and constructed laboratories and classrooms. To meet expenses, the Prince supplemented government money with his own funds as well as taking donations from other members of the Royal Family. He even took a hands-on role, teaching vertebrate anatomy.

Recognising the need to upgrade the quality of qualified teaching staff, Prince Mahidol provided scholarships for six students to travel to England and study chemistry, biology and physics.

These students returned to Siam and set about imparting their knowledge and experience to others, thereby lifting the overall standards and providing a core of homegrown talent in the basic sciences.

To further enhance the standard of public health, Prince Mahidol was appointed Chairman of the Committee to establish the Siriraj School of Medicine in Bangkok.

Suffering from kidney problems, Prince Mahidol and his family travelled to Heidelberg in Germany to seek treatment. In 1925, his second child, Prince Ananda Mahidol (later to become King Rama VIII) was born.

After leaving Germany, the family went to the United States where Prince Mahidol resumed his medical studies at Harvard University.

It was while in the United States that his third child, Prince Bhumibol Adulyadej (later King Rama IX) was born, in Cambridge, Massachusetts on 5 December 1927.

Prince Mahidol received a well-earned Doctor of Medicine degree in 1928 and immediately returned to Siam with his family, determined to use his medical knowledge for the betterment of his people.

At the newly opened Siriraj School of Medicine, he taught final year medical students, exhorting them to not only be a doctor, "...but I also want you to be a human being".

The Prince also taught at the fledgling Chulalongkorn University, and took a keen interest in its development, donating his own funds for lecturers and scholarships and co-ordinating assistance from the Rockefeller Foundation to the university.

He proposed that Chulalongkorn University be autonomous and separated from the Ministry of Education and be given the freedom to formulate both academic and administrative policies as well as manage its own financial affairs.

A former student who studied under the Prince, recalled "[He] was a person who mixed freely with commoners. He enjoyed the company of his students and was not one to put himself above anyone."

However, due to his Royal status, he was not allowed to serve as an intern. Disappointed at this restriction, Prince Mahidol left his family behind in Bangkok and went north to work as a resident doctor in Chiang Mai at the McCormick Hospital, run by American missionaries under Dr. E. Court.

Prince Mahidol performed operations alongside Dr. Court, living up to his statement that, "Real success exists not in learning but in its application for the benefit of mankind."

In August 1929, Prince Mahidol travelled to Bangkok to attend a funeral. He never returned.

Prince Mahidol's kidney problems, despite treatment in Germany and elsewhere had never really dissipated and gradually become quite serious, to such an extent he never told his family the true extent of his illness. Prince Mahidol died in Bangkok on 24 September at the age of 37 of, among other things, amoebic liver abscess.

While laid low with this fatal illness, he had written a will leaving 500,000 baht to the medical school and Siriraj Hospital. The income from this fund was to be used in sending doctors, nurses, and pharmacists abroad to further their medical education.

Known by the appellation, 'Father of Thai Medicine and Public Health', in 1992 Prince Mahidol of Songkhla was named by UNESCO as an Eminent Educator, Scientist and Humanist.

Siam's First Foreign-Produced Feature Film

In the early years of the 1920s the adventurous and innovative Canadian-born, American-based film producer, director and screenwriter Henry MacRae came to Siam. After obtaining the consent and assistance of local authorities, MacRae made the first feature-length film by a Hollywood studio in Siam and starring an all-Siamese cast. Titled *Miss Suwanna of Siam* it premiered in June 1923, but not without attracting local controversy. Sadly, the two copies of the 35mm silent film left in Siam have been lost, or possibly intentionally destroyed, and no copy of it exists among the American archives.

Henry MacRae in 1921

Born in Toronto in Canada in 1876, Henry MacRae began making movies and serials during the silent era in Hollywood from 1912 onwards. He is credited with a number of innovations from using artificial light for interiors, to shooting at night, the wind machine and double exposure. His output eventually exceeded 130 films and included *Tarzan the Tiger,* the first Tarzan movie with sound, made in 1929, the *Flash Gordon* serial (1936) and his final movie *Flash Gordon Conquers the Universe,* made in 1940, the year MacRae died.

In 1922 he travelled to Southeast Asia. After making a film in the southern Philippines he came to Bangkok to do the same for

Universal Studios. His first task was to obtain government permission to make the film, which would star local actors.

In an article entitled 'Picturesque and Unusual Siam' that appeared in the 1924 edition of the *Film Yearbook*, MacRae wrote,

His Majesty The King, is a graduate of Oxford, England, and believes he is a second Shakespeare, that is the Shakespeare of Siam. He spends a great amount of his time translating Shakespeare into Siamese and producing these dramas and comedies with his own people- actors from what they call The Royal Entertainment Company. These actors, both men and women, are adopted into the Royal Entertainment Company when they are children and have a life-long job. They receive a satisfactory salary and their expenses for living, and are all given titles, after they reach a certain age. I felt that His Majesty would be interested in moving pictures, and after considerable maneuvering I finally secured an audience which resulted in securing the entire company's assistance together with the free use of the King's 52 automobiles. His Majesty's 600 race horses, the free use of the navy, the Royal Palaces, the railways, the rice mills, thousands of miles of rice fields, cocoanut groves, klongs and Elephants, and white elephants at that. The white elephant of which we have heard so much, is on close inspection not even light colored; the only distinction being a number of white spots on their ears and having white eyes. But they are a very sacred proposition with the King and the natives, and every white elephant discovered is the property of the King, and is given a special palace to live in with a number of attendants, and always has the association of a pure white monkey.

A prince of the Royal Court noted in his diary, 'Today Mr Henry A. MacRae came to see me. I assured him of two things: first, travelling; second, finding a place for film processing and screening. Above these, he has to take care of himself. For our benefit, he has to give a copy of the film to the State Railway in return...' At that time it fell to the Royal State Railways to oversee such diversities as films and the promotion of tourism. When the film was completed, MacRae did indeed give a copy to the State Railways, as well as one to King Vajiravudh.

The film itself was a romance, written and directed by MacRae, with Robert Kerr as assistant director. Kerr would return to Siam in

1928 to direct *The White Rose,* a film shown in Bangkok in September that year.

The two lead actors in *Miss Suwanna of Siam* were Sa-ngaim Naveesatien as the heroine Suwanna, and Ram Projtasart as her love interest. As MacRae later noted, 'The women of Siam are rather a fine looking lot some of them very attractive and always very clean in dress and manner.' Suwanna suffers her father's disapproval but eventually finds true love as well as filial reconciliation. Although it was basically a standard romance MacRae and his film crew apparently used every opportunity to include as much exotic footage as possible, most of it in Bangkok.

'We managed to secure some very excellent scenes of the King in action and also his Prime Minister. The most interesting features of Bangkok…are its wonderful temples or watts (sic) as they are called. The temples cover about 30 acres of ground and are built of stone and brick, and decorated with gold leaf and inlaid with mother of pearl. A form of Siamese worship is to paste a piece of gold leaf on some part of the temple, even the outside of the wall that surrounds the watt. The native priests are peculiar looking fellows with shaved heads and dressed in long yellow cloaks. They are called priests of the Yellow Robe and are not allowed to keep any money that they may receive, longer than 24 hours.'

Of the filming in Siam MacRae wrote, 'One of the interesting features of making a picture with the Royal actors was that they would become very serious in the work but if any counter attraction occurred they would all disappear. On one occasion I had a long scene all rehearsed and started to shoot. When the principal character actor was supposed to come into the scene he was nowhere in sight. I finally discovered that he was taking a bath.'

The film title, in Thai, has been variously written as *Nangsao Suwan, Nang Sao Suwan* or *Nong Sao Suwan.* In spite of the existence of the Thai General System of Transcription for transliteration of Thai into English, the eponymous lead character in the film has been written variously as Suwan, Suwann, Suwarn, Suwarna, Suvarn, and Suvarna. Two alternate titles of the film include *The Gold of Siam* and *Kingdom of Heaven.*

'When our picture was finished the King had it presented in his palace with his entire court in attendance. He was delighted with it, and as the titles were in English he showed his extreme cleverness in translating the titles into Siamese as the picture was being shown. The whole court greatly admired the picture and we were given a decoration,' MacRae stated in his *Film Review* piece.

MacRae's movie had its premiere on Friday night 22 June 1923 at the Nakhon Sri Thammarat theatre. The Monday 25 June edition of the *Bangkok Daily Mail* newspaper carried the following report on the second night screening:

On Saturday night last, there were record attendances to witness the film 'Suvarna of Siam' *and incidentally to aid in support of the Siam* Red *Cross, the management having most generously undertaken to give all the takings to that most excellent institution.*

H.R.H. *Admiral the Prince of Nakhon Ratchasima was present at the Phathanakorn, where a most excellent programme was provided.*

Naturally an immense amount of interest centered upon 'Suvarna of Siam' *the local drama-film upon which Mr. Henry Macrae, Mr. Robert Kerr and Mr. Dal Clawson have been at work for some time past. The film is of special interest as it is the first big thing of the kind ever made in this country and it has been so constructed as to afford the greatest collection possible of scenic backgrounds, thus affording a sort of panorama of the country with the story of Suvarna running through it all, like the leit motif of an opera. The story itself has all the necessary features of melodrama, love, hate, revenge, injured innocence, false accusation, man-slaughter, etc., etc., and it all ends up nicely and pleasantly with the long-lost heir coming to his own and the lovers wandering off hand in hand into the bright future.*

And all this wanders through a lot of real life scenes, from Their Royal Highnesses the Princes Damrong and Purachatra sitting "at the receipt of custom" to "elephants a pilin' teak," golf at Hua Hin, the Raek Na ceremony, a Bangkok fire, and views upon views of palaces and wats, incidentally proving a really first-class advertisement to the State Railways and various other of Siam's modernities.

The film is certainly well worth seeing, from the scenic standpoint alone and all concerned in its production merit all credit for good work well done. It will be shown tonight again at the Phathanakorn and Hong Kong cinemas and we certainly advise all who have not seen it to do so.

Prior to its release, it has been suggested a censorship committee ordered the cutting of scenes in which a real prisoner was executed. If this is true it appears very strange that a journalist writing in the *Sambhand Thai* newspaper is quoted, 'I would like to blame the local officer who did not save the honour of the country by forbidding them to do so. The execution will represent the barbarism of Siam.' Surely this suggests the finished product retained the execution scenes.

It may well be this controversy concerning the execution scenes led to the copies of the film disappearing: perhaps simply discarded or intentionally let deteriorate.

Although it was apparently intended for show outside Siam, there is no evidence of any overseas screening, either in the United States or anywhere else. Given the expenses involved, the film must have proved a financial flop. Three screenings over just three days could not possibly have recovered costs.

All that exists of the film today is some promotional material held at the Thailand National Film Archive.

Thailand's contribution to the land campaigns of the United Nations in the Korean War

In the early hours of a rainy Sunday, 25 June 1950, heavily armed military units from the Democratic People's Republic of Korea (North Korea) launched an invasion of the Republic of Korea (South Korea). The action heralded the beginning of a protracted conflict that was to last for just over three years.

Two days later, as the South Korean (ROK) defence forces crumbled and fell back, the UN Security Council met in hurried session and agreed to '…furnish such assistance to the Republic of Korea as may be necessary to repel the armed attack and to restore international peace and security to the area.'

By-passing Congress, US President Harry Truman ordered the commander-in-chief of the Far East, General Douglas Macarthur, to provide whatever assistance was needed to repel the North Korean invasion. By referring to the conflict as a 'police action' instead of a full-blown 'war', Truman was able, under the articles of the US Constitution, to justify his direct intervention rather than wait for Congress to give its assent.

American forces based in occupied Japan were airlifted into South Korea and went into action for the first time on 5 July. Outnumbered and outgunned, the small South Korean army and the US forces fought delaying actions, aiming to gain the necessary time for more US reinforcements to arrive and for other UN member states to commit troops to the battlefield.

Britain was the first nation to agree to join the US in Korea, followed in rapid succession by Australia, France, Canada, and New Zealand. The first forces from these nations began arriving in southern Korea in late August.

On 20 July 1950, following a late-night meeting lasting more than three hours by the members of the Defence Board of Thailand, an agreement was reached to offer a 4,000-strong contingent to support the UN effort. Prime Minister Pibul Songgram was quoted as saying, "Only by fast and decisive action can we cope with the critical situation all over Asia." This was an oblique reference to the recent fall of China to the Communists as well as the on-going revolts against French rule in Vietnam and Laos and the largely expatriate Chinese insurgency in Malaya.

That April, the United States had allocated more than $10 million worth of arms and other military equipment specifically designed to combat the so-called 'communist menace'. Money was also allocated for the construction of highways, especially for the north-east region of Thailand. This allocation further brought Thailand into the American sphere of influence, despite the large numbers of Chinese immigrants who made up a high proportion of the Thai population.

Thailand's first measure of support for South Korea had come on 30 June when she sent four tonnes of rice as a goodwill gesture.

The UN and US officially accepted Thailand's offer off troops for Korea on 16 August, the first by an Asian nation. Significantly, Thailand's offer gave the lie to a claim by the Soviet Union that only European countries would send soldiers to fight in Korea. The Thai ambassador to the United States, Prince Wan Waithayakon stated Thai forces were being committed "to defend the cause of peace, freedom and justice. Aggression must be stopped in Korea, or anywhere else, otherwise small nations will fall." Although he stated Thai soldiers would be sent as soon as possible, it would be almost two months before the first troops were ready to embark.

In September, the Philippines joined the UN coalition, becoming the first Asian country to put its soldiers on the ground in Korea. The coalition eventually encompassed 16 nations, with South Africa, the Netherlands, Greece, Belgium, Luxembourg, Ethiopia, Turkey and Colombia, committing troops to the United Nations Command (UNC), as the intervention force was known. Additionally, Denmark, India, Norway and Sweden provided medical units and Italy, although not a member of the UN, supplied a hospital.

A newspaper report filed by the AAP-Reuter correspondent in Bangkok suggested the imminent arrival of the Thai Expeditionary Force (TEF) should 'not be underrated' claiming the Thais would 'likely [prove] a first-class small-arms fighting unit.' The reporter noted the UN could expect a Thai soldier to possess three qualities: 'imagination, patriotism, and personal bravery.' It was noted the TEF was a voluntary force and 'when the government called for 4,000 men, 14,000 volunteered within a fortnight.' Among those volunteers was Prince Chalermpol, who was assigned the rank of a captain in the infantry.

A small advance force of Thai troops arrived in Japan on 12 October. Eight days later a ceremony for 1,200 Thai infantrymen took place in Bangkok with a parade down Ratchadamnoen Avenue, reviewed by Army Commander-in-Chief General Phin Choonhavan. The commander told his men Communism was a menace which needed to be stopped, which is why Thai troops were now on their way to help in the defence of South Korea. This would be the first occasion Thai troops had served overseas since the First World War.

The first contingent of Thai soldiers, designated the 21st Infantry Regiment, arrived in South Korea on 7 November. The Thais were initially assigned to the US 187th Airborne Regiment, then to I Corps (December 1950), IX Corps (January 1951), the 1st Cavalry Division (March 1951) and finally the 2nd Infantry Division (27 December 1951).

The Thai troops arrived during the coldest winter for two centuries. Despite the intensely cold weather, Thai morale was boosted by the arrival of 10 specialist cooks who provided traditional Thai cuisine to the soldiers.

Thai Soldiers arrived at Pusan in 1950
Credit Republic of Korea Armed Forces CC BY-SA 2.0
https://commons.wikimedia.org/w/index.php?curid=36999548

The Thais did not see action until almost four months after their arrival. In cold conditions, this first combat took place on 28 February 1951 near Hoengsong on the central front. Assisting their ROK allies, the Thai troops, led by Colonel Boriboon Chulacharita, engaged the North Koreans in a two-hour battle. The Thais and ROK soldiers attacked the North Koreans in a two-pronged assault. The action ended with success, the Thais and ROK claiming 50 North Koreans killed and dozens wounded. The Thais suffered one man wounded.

While operating with the US 1st Cavalry Division, the Thai contingent impressed their allies with a strong performance in action near Uijongbu, some 30 kilometres northeast of Seoul. This was after the unofficial Chinese entry into the war which saw UN forces hurled back from the North Korea-China border. The action was prior to Seoul falling for the second time.

A UN counter-offensive recovered Seoul and by the end of April 1951 the front line was established and maintained around the 38th Parallel, the pre-war boundary between the two Koreas.

On 2 June, the Thais, along with Greek, Turkish, and Philippine troops, and heavily supported by US artillery, tanks and air strikes, fought a successful eight-day battle to secure what was known as the Chorwon-Kumhwa area, approximately 32 kilometres inside North Korea.

Soon after this victory the conflict developed into a stalemate which became eerily reminiscent of the Western Front of the First World War. What had previously been a series of lengthy advances and equally lengthy withdrawals settled into a series of main line positions with artillery duels outweighing small arms engagements.

Between 31 July and 7 September 1951, Thai troops assisted the US 1st Cavalry Division and other UN units with the defence of Yuldong (Yultong), north of Yeoncheon. This was soon after peace talks had commenced and rumours of a settlement 'within weeks' constantly swept through the lines. From mid-1951 until the end of the war the UNC followed a policy of attempting to hold the main battle line rather than trying to achieve an all-out military victory.

For the Thais, the harsh Korean winters were harder to endure than the numerous Chinese and North Korean frontal assaults and artillery and mortar barrages made against their section of the UN line. Most of the men had never seen snow and a number fell victim to frostbite.

By the second winter (1951-1952) the Thais were supplied with American winter clothing and equipment and their officers given ready-made log bunkers for use as command posts. A group of 200 Thai replacement soldiers for those who had suffered frostbite as well as battle wounds were given intensive cold weather training alongside their American compatriots.

For the Thai land forces, perhaps their finest performance came in October and November 1952. The 21st Infantry Regiment replaced an American regiment on Hill 255, which was better known as Pork Chop Hill due to its shape. Hill 255 was one of six peaks which had been secured by the UN as part of a buffer for their line. The Chinese and North Koreans decided that it, and a number of other hills, needed to be recaptured. According to the official history of the US 2nd Division, 'Enemy probes on this outpost were regularly repelled by the defenders in the first few days of November. These probes grew in size and were supported by intense artillery and mortar fire. The climax came on the night of 10 November when an enemy battalion made repeated attacks on Pork Chop throughout the night. Several groups of Chinese reached the trenches of the Thailanders but the outpost was never lost. A Thai patrol cleared the slopes of any remaining Communists by morning of the 11th. Probes of smaller size continued to hit Pork Chop in the succeeding days and were driven off each time.' An estimated 800 Chinese troops were killed over the nights of 10 and 11 November.

With the ground covered in snow, the most significant operations over the next month or so were patrols designed to defend against Chinese infiltration. The Chinese launched a company-sized attack on 21 December, but again the Thai line held firm. When they were relieved by an American formation, the US soldiers found the departing Thais had written 'take good care of our Pork Chop' on one of the walls of the wooden bunkers.

In a separate incident, Major Alvin Price, the American commander of a battalion in the 2nd Infantry Division, was travelling in a jeep in South Korea with other soldiers, including the commander of a Thai battalion, when they came under mortar fire. They stopped the jeep and took cover in a ditch, all except the Thai commander. Price, a Second World War veteran, left his cover and, in his words, "…went back and got him and pulled him over into the ditch." Soon after he left the army in 1953, Price was awarded the Order of the Crown of Thailand by a grateful Thai government.

Through January and February 1953, the Thai battalion 'had an especially high number of contacts with Chinese patrols and probes.'

One of the last actions for the Thais began on 13 July 1953 at Hill 351 and became known as the battle of Kumhwa. A series of Chinese assaults against the position were beaten back over the next two weeks as armistice talks neared an end.

Finally, on 27 July 1953 after lengthy negotiations, an armistice was signed at Panmunjon. Both sides agreed to retire a distance of two kilometres from the last line of military contact, thereby creating a Demilitarised Zone (DMZ). Large numbers of US and UN troops, among them elements of the TEF, remained in South Korea to provide defence and act as a deterrent to further North Korean and Chinese aggression.

On 31 January 1955 more than 800 Thai soldiers and sailors arrived in Bangkok from South Korea. Large crowds were at the port to welcome the troops home after their service with UN and ROK forces.

When Prime Minister Pibul Songgram addressed the returnees he stated, "It is necessary to withdraw the Thai Expeditionary Force, because the situation around our own country requires careful watching."

All told, the TEF consisted of three infantry battalions, four naval vessels, and one air transport company. Over the 33 months the TEF spent fighting in Korea these units lost 91 men killed in battle. Another 27 died of other causes and 794 had been wounded or injured. Five men were missing. Additionally, apart from the United

States, Thailand was one of 10 other nations to send nurses to serve with the UNC.

A special cremation ceremony for the 118 men who died in Korea took place on 24 March 1955, presided over by King Bhumibol Adulyadej.

On 22 June 1972 the last 157 Thai troops left South Korea, completing almost 22 years of help in the military defence of that country. All told, around 18,500 Thai military personnel served tours of duty in Korea between 1950 and 1972.

Return of the Generals: the coup of 1947

On 8 November 1947, officers calling themselves the 'Coup Group' launched a bloodless putsch which overthrew the government of prime minister Admiral Thamrong Nawasawat and abrogated the 1946 Constitution. It was the first successful coup attempt since 1939.

Led by Lieutenant-General Phin Choonhavan and General Phao Sriyanond, with the support of former prime minister Field Marshal Pibul Songgram, the Coup Group launched their putsch at 2:00am.

General Phin Choonhavan

No shots were fired and the transition proved as smooth as any armed takeover of a government could.

The coup leaders, many of them veterans of the 1942 Shan States campaign, claimed they had taken action to protect royal prestige and end corruption. They claimed the Thamrong government was responsible for costing Siam more than 100 million baht due to corrupt practices and activities. Among other leading members of the

Coup Group were Air Force commander Fuen Ronnaphagrad and Army Colonel Sarit Thanarat.

Although Khuang Aphaiwong was installed as interim prime minister, it was an open secret the real power lay with Pibul Songgram.

After announcing elections would take place in January 1948, a temporary constitution was promulgated and approved by the Regent, Prince Rangsit, just a day after the coup.

Rumours of a potential coup and return to power by Pibul and his clique had been circulating Bangkok for months. The intense rivalry between Pibul and former premier Pridi Banomyong and his supporters effectively split the country, much like the Yellow Shirt-Red Shirt troubles would plague the nation six decades later.

At the end of the Second World War, it was Pridi and his Free Thai Movement compatriots who held the ascendancy. The mysterious death of King Ananda Mahidol in June 1946 plunged Siam into a period of deep uncertainty, fuelled by rumours of high-level involvement in the unexplained demise.

The speculation led to the resignation of Pridi as prime minister and the appointment of Thamrong Nawasawat in his stead.

Pibul was viewed with suspicion and even hostility by the United States, Britain and other allies who had fought the Japanese.

At the end of March, Pibul had claimed Siam needed him to continue the march towards democracy which he had begun to implement during his 1939-1944 premiership. Pibul had formed a new political party called Tharmathipat (Right is Might) and he said its platform included a number of democratic reforms.

At the same time, Pibul was charged by the government with claiming unauthorised expenditures during his time in power. He was ordered to pay back over one million baht for using government funds to repair his official residence, for fuel and entertainment expenses and an unexplained 'special secret service' fee.

The British government, by way of their Information Service, made it clear they had not forgotten it was under Pibul 'that Siam declared war on the British and American democracies.'

A month before Pibul made his announcement, Pridi returned from a four-month trip to the United States and Europe. A crowd estimated at over 10,000 welcomed Pridi and his wife Poonsuk as they stepped ashore from a flying boat at Klong Toey in Bangkok. Among those on hand to welcome Pridi home was prime minister Thamrong.

While in the United States, Pridi became one of the first recipients of the US Medal of Freedom. The award had been created by President Harry Truman in 1945 and was one of the highest awards a civilian could receive. The award was made 'for meritorious services during the war as leader of the…resistance movement against the Japanese in Siam.'

Pibul worked at creating the kind of 'spin' for which politicians the world over are renowned. In May he told Captain David Parsons, an American military officer who was in Bangkok to collect evidence for the trial of alleged Japanese war criminals in Tokyo, that Siam was never really a genuine ally of Japan.

Pibul claimed he only declared war on Britain and the United States to save the lives and property of the citizens of those countries living in Siam. In a three-hour interview with Parsons, Pibul claimed the Japanese intended to confiscate British and US property in Siam as well as arrest and kill citizens of the two countries. He said by allying with Japan, Siam was able to take custody of both property and people, thereby saving lives.

On 28 May, Prime Minister Thamrong and his cabinet resigned following a series of scandals. The worst of these had been the purchase of 18 American-made Buick's for cabinet members, a luxury Siam could ill-afford. In attempt to divert criticism, five of the luxury vehicles were given to regional army commanders.

Despite the resignation, no one else could form a government, so Thamrong was invited to return and put together a new cabinet.

In August, the parliament passed an anti-corruption bill after Thamrong gave an assurance its provisions would be firmly enforced, no matter who was caught up in the net. The new act of parliament would later be used by his rivals against some of Thamrong's own ministers and officials.

In October, two women being held by the police on defamation charges, claimed they received bribes of 200,000 baht to spread rumours about Pridi, specifically his alleged involvement in the death of King Ananda in 1946. They told police an 'influential person' paid them to perform this task in the hope of undermining Pridi's government. Police suggested they would soon be arresting a number of well-known persons in connection with the women's claims.

A month later the Coup Group executed its putsch. Although the takeover was relatively peaceful, troops had been sent to seize Pridi at his riverside residence. It is even suggested the troops were sent to kill him. As an armoured vehicle smashed through the gates of his compound, Pridi escaped by boat and obtained refuge in the naval headquarters alongside the Chao Phraya River.

Pridi had great support within the navy and was sheltered by Admiral Sindhu Songkhramchai. Ousted prime minister Admiral Thamrong also sought shelter inside the base.

On the night of 10 November, Pridi and Thamrong were secretly visited by a senior British adviser and an American diplomat. Pridi told the men he regarded Admiral Thamrong's government as legal and constitutional and from the naval base they would attempt to rally support for a possible counter-coup. Pridi stressed no counter-coup would be undertaken until he could be 'reasonably certain' of success, and he knew this would take some time.

Admiral Thamrong stated if they reached the conclusion their chances of a counter-coup would not be successful, he would surrender to Pibul, as he did not believe his life was in any real danger.

Thamrong felt this way after assurances had been conveyed by the Siamese naval attaché to the British naval attaché Captain Stratford Dennis claiming Pibul would not harm the ousted prime minister.

Pridi said he 'would have to leave the country as he was convinced that once captured, his life would be in grave danger. He therefore asked that in the event British authorities would facilitate his escape to Malaya or other British territory.'

Both the British and the Americans made it clear to Pridi that neither government would be likely to sanction the use of force to help him regain power. Neither country wished to become militarily embroiled in the internal troubles of Siam.

In the week following the coup, the new regime made unsubstantiated accusations that Pridi was the mastermind of a Communist plot to murder King Ananda.

Realising his position was becoming increasingly untenable, Pridi arrived at the Bangkok residence of Captain Dennis just before dawn on 19 November.

The Senior Statesman, as he was referred to by both the British and the Americans, Pridi was wearing a naval uniform and thick glasses, had grown a moustache and removed his false teeth in an attempt to disguise himself.

He told the attaché he had spent the night at Thonburi talking with the Marines and realised the coup leaders' attempts at involving him in the death of the monarch the previous year had 'lost him much support in and out of the Navy…'

Pridi then asked if the British would help him escape Siam. The British Ambassador, Geoffrey Thompson, knew he was not in a position to help Pridi and his family leave the country, so he contacted Edwin Stanton, the US Ambassador, to ask for assistance.

Thompson and Stanton came up with a trio of options for leaving the country. First, Pridi could arrange for the Siamese navy to hire a Cathay Airways Catalina flying boat. Second, a request could be made to Pibul to allow Pridi and his family to leave as ordinary passengers on a British Overseas Aircraft Corporation (BOAC) flight from Don Muang. The third and final option was 'for the family to be taken out to sea beyond territorial limits by a Naval launch there to embark on a merchant vessel bound for Singapore.'

Pridi flatly refused the second option and settled on the third.

A Shell Company tanker was sailing that day and 'her master has been told by the local manager that if hailed on the high seas, he may accede to the request for onward transportation, ' wrote Thompson in a diplomatic cable to the British Foreign Office and marked 'secret.'

As Ambassador Thompson noted in his report, 'I disliked all this dangerous melodrama, but neither United States Ambassador nor I can see how else we can act. We are handicapped from every point of view, and the sooner these people get out and away the better.'

Stanton authorised the US naval attaché Commander Skeats Gardas to take Pridi and his family back down the river. Leaving the US naval attache's residence Pridi 'Left behind…two or three machine guns, several other weapons and two hand-grenades,' wrote Thompson in a later report. 'These will be disposed of discreetly,' the British ambassador concluded.

After making it safely back to his residence, Pridi began organizing himself, family and entourage for the more risky task of exiting Siam.

He determined not to risk bringing his family with him to Singapore. Instead, his wife and five children were sent to the relative safety of the Sattahip naval base, on the eastern seaboard south of Bangkok.

On the night of 19 November, Gardas, assisted by his wife and sister, collected Pridi, his secretary, a Siamese police bodyguard and a servant, and sailed 60 kilometres out into the Gulf of Thailand to rendezvous with the Shell tanker.

After Pridi and his assistants were safely put aboard the tanker, Gardas attempted to return to Bangkok. The weather was rough and his sailing vessel had to lay up on a sandbank.

Early the following morning, a Siamese officer called on the United States military attache and informed him Commander Gardas had been seen to embark 'three naval officers one of whom has been recognised as one of those wanted on suspicion of having been concerned in the death of the late King.'

The Siamese officer wanted to know the whereabouts of Gardas and his vessel and asked the US military attaché to deputise a senior US military officer to accompany a proposed search.

The attaché told the Siamese officer he would need to speak first with Edwin Stanton. By the time he had done so, Gardas and his boat were safely back in Bangkok. The Siamese officer was told Gardas had been on a 'fishing trip'.

Naturally, the British ambassador was well aware 'The news is…bound to break sooner or later and there will…be a [diplomatic] row,' wrote Thompson. 'I would view this event with complete equanimity were it not for Senior Statesman having been accompanied by his secretary. It is fortunate that no…formal charges have ever been brought against this individual.'

For his part, Pridi made three requests of the British and Americans. The first was 'to assist his wife and family to leave the country.' The second, 'That authorities at Singapore should make no…difficulty about entry of himself and his friends into the Colony,' and, finally, 'that on arrival he might be provided with funds as he had none.'

Ambassador Thompson asked the Singapore authorities to help with the second and third requests, but in relation to helping Pridi's family leave Siam, 'United States Ambassador and I are agreed that it would be inadvisable for either of us to take any initiative anyway for the time being.'

Recognizing the strong likelihood the new Siamese government would be well aware of the British and US involvement in Pridi's escape, Thompson wrote, 'Should I be tackled about…Pridi's escape I would propose to take the following line…(a) that whatever his political opponents may think he took grave risks for the Allies during the war and consequently has earned our gratitude. (b) that he took sanctuary with us when in danger and could not…be betrayed. (c) that so far as I knew he is not charged with any crime and (d) that in facilitating his departure after had ordered his "Free Siamese" to return home, we have contributed to the maintenance of internal order. United States Ambassador will do the same…'

Ambassador Thompson's diplomatic calm had been tested to its limits during the days following the coup. As he noted, both Britain and the United States felt they owed Pridi a debt for his service during the Second World War. Even so, it's easy to see he was happy when Pridi was finally out of Siam. As he noted in a telegram which was classified as 'of particular secrecy' and sent late on the morning of 19 November, 'I think you will probably agree that by our action today my United States colleague and I have discharged our humanitarian and other obligations towards…Pridi.' He concluded,

'So far as I am concerned he will have to paddle his own canoe thenceforth.'

In a minor sequel, on 27 November, troops loyal to the new government fired shots at Pridi's Chao Phrya River residence, not realising he had already left the country. Or perhaps they did, and wanted to produce a token show of force, sending a subtle but clear message to Pridi and his supporters in that most Asian of ways.

The Senior Statesman would remain in exile for the next 15 months.

Thailand's reluctant role in the *Mayaguez* incident

Just two weeks after the collapse of South Vietnam completed the rout of American arms in the Second Indochina War, the United States was faced with what it called an 'act of piracy' by the newly-installed Khmer Rouge regime in Cambodia when the 10,000-ton container ship SS *Mayaguez* was stopped and seized by a Cambodian patrol boat.

The old and unarmed American container ship was allegedly cruising 100 kilometres offshore on her way to Sattahip in Thailand from Hong Kong when she was stopped and impounded in the early afternoon of 12 May 1975. It was precisely a month since American forces had evacuated the US ambassador, his staff and others as Phnom Penh fell to Khmer Rouge.

The Cambodians claimed the *Mayaguez* was a spy ship. President Gerald Ford decided the US needed to send a message to the rest of the world that his nation had not turned into a 'paper tiger' and orders were issued to send troops and naval forces to the area and prepare to effect the rescue of Captain Charles Miller, the skipper of the *Mayaguez*, and his crew of 39 men. Ford expected diplomatic efforts to gain the release of the crew and ship would fail and wanted to be in a position as quickly as possible to take decisive military action.

On 13 May the *Mayaguez* was been taken to Koh Tang, an island 54 kilometres off the Cambodian coast, where she was kept under constant surveillance US military aircraft based in Thailand and the Philippines.

Although Ford had become the only unelected US president in history, following the resignation in August 1974 of Richard Nixon, he was a man who had been a fervent supporter of the war in Vietnam.

In 1965, Ford said, "If we give up in South Vietnam, it would give up Southeast Asia, and our defence lines would be driven back to the Hawaiian islands." Having only been able to watch as Cambodia and South Vietnam fell to the Communists, Ford saw the seizure of the *Mayaguez* as an opportunity to restore some much needed prestige.

American military personnel were still at a number of bases in Thailand and the US angered the Kukrit Pramoj government by unilaterally taking the decision to send a battalion of marines from Okinawa (other sources suggest they came from Subic Bay in the Philippines) to the U-Tapao airbase. From here they would be flown the 312 kilometres to Koh Tang and attempt to rescue the *Mayaguez* crew.

Sadly, operations began badly for the Americans when 23 security police and crew from their base at Nakhom Phanom were killed in a helicopter crash west of the town on 13 May.

On 14 May - unbeknownst to the Americans - the crew of the *Mayaguez* had been transferred by fishing boat to an island at the entrance to the port of Sihanoukville, then called Kompong Som. On the same day, US air force jets sank three Cambodian gunboats.

The rescue attempt was arranged for the early morning of 15 May with 227 marines boarding 11 air force helicopters at U-Tapao. They left for Cambodia at around 3:00am.

Under fighter cover, 179 marines landed on Koh Tang, some on the western side of the island, the remainder on the east. The Americans had seriously underestimated the Cambodian military presence on Koh Tang and came under heavy fire. Two helicopters were shot down early, with the loss of 13 men. Another 13 men swam out to sea and were eventually rescued by the destroyer USS *Henry B Wilson*.

A third helicopter landed on the beach, its tail shot off. The troops formed a defensive perimeter and held off a number of Cambodian attacks.

In the meantime, three helicopters dropped 48 marines and 12 sailors onto the deck of the destroyer escort USS *Harold E Holt*. The warship then went alongside *Mayaguez* and the marines boarded the empty container ship.

On the western side of Koh Tang, one helicopter was seriously damaged and had to limp back to the coast of Thailand. A second helicopter landed troops but when it took off again it crashed into the sea with the loss of one crewman. Further helicopters landed more marines, with one group of 29 men being forced to disembark to the south.

Unknown to the troops, the crew of the *Mayaguez* had been inexplicably released by the Khmer Rouge earlier that morning for reasons that were never forthcoming. They were placed aboard a previously captured Thai fishing boat and, together with the Thais, sailed out to the USS *Henry B Wilson,* arriving at around 10:00am.

A second wave of 127 marines, aboard five helicopters, were on their way to Koh Tang when they heard of the release. They turned back to U-Tapao but then were ordered to again head for Koh Tang by the operation commander.

Four of the helicopters landed and disgorged marines; the fifth was hit by gunfire and retreated to Thailand where it made an emergency landing. With 225 US troops on Koh Tang orders were issued to organize an evacuation.

US Marines on Koh Tang, 1975

Around this time, planes from the aircraft carrier USS *Coral Sea* struck the Ream Air Force base, destroying about 17 Cambodian aircraft. A second wave bombed the Ream Naval base and an inactive oil refinery at Sihanoukville.

Over the next eight hours, helicopters managed to extract everybody except three marines. In all the confusion surrounding the various attacks and landings, as well as the dislocation in the chain of command, no one realised there were three men unaccounted for until it was too late.

Although various theories regarding the fate of the three have been propounded over the years, the truth is that no one knows what happened to them. In all likelihood they had already been either captured or killed before the last marines left Koh Tang.

All told, the US lost 41 men killed and 50 wounded in the *Mayaguez* incident, including the 23 air force men tragically lost in Thailand at the outset of the whole affair.

A consequence of the failure of President Ford to ask the Thais if the US could use their bases for the *Mayaguez* rescue was an anti-American demonstration in front of the US embassy on 17 May by an estimated 10,000 students and activists led by Thirayuth Boonmee. The brass American eagle was ripped off the front gate and thrown into the street.

Echoing the protesters, the Kukrit Pramoj government demanded an official apology from the US for flying marines into U-Tapao without permission. Foreign Minister Chatichai Choonhavan said Anand Panyarachun, the Thai ambassador to the US, would be withdrawn while the government awaited a response and all treaties between the two countries would be reviewed.

Two days later, the United States issued an official apology but the 3,000 or so protesters still outside the American embassy demanded all US forces be withdrawn from Thailand. In March 1976, Kukrit gave the US 18 months to remove its troops from the country. They were gone by December that year.

The beginnings of the Postal Service

The world's first post office was established in Britain in 1619 and in 1840, regular mail received a boost when the first commercial postage stamp was issued. In Siam, prior to the establishment of an organised postal service, internal messages were divided into two classes: ordinary and urgent. An ordinary message was delivered by a regular, but slow, service from province to province. A special courier conveyed urgent messages as fast as possible.

Changes were implemented in the message and letter delivery system. Initially, major cities and towns were staffed with regular couriers, meaning, for example, that a Bangkok courier need only go as far as Saraburi where he handed his mail on. The message would then continue to each major city or town by regular courier until it reached its destination, a very slow and laborious process.

Ordinary correspondence destined for overseas was entrusted to traders who were going in the direction of the letters or messages in question. Hardly a regular or even efficient method of maintaining contact with the outside world. If no traders could be found, special messengers had to be employed for the task. Important correspondence was necessarily handled by specially employed couriers.

All foreign mail destined for Siam arrived under an arrangement with the British-controlled Straits Settlements in Singapore and Hong Kong. The British Consulate in Bangkok acted as the intermediary.

In 1875, the government decided to begin the distribution of its newspaper *Court* to citizens in Bangkok, rather than require them to come to an office in the Grand Palace and pick it up. Stamps were attached to the wrapper of the newspaper and couriers were hired to deliver *Court* to subscribers. This marked the beginning of a postal service.

By 1876, stamps were being used for letters to subscribers and delivered by mail carriers. The cost of a stamp was one Att, approximately three satang. For deliveries within Bangkok, the price was one Att, anywhere outside the city it doubled to two Att.

Court failed soon after and with its demise, stamps and postmen also became redundant.

However, four years later the issue of a postal service was again raised and in 1881 King Chulalongkorn noted that '...the introduction of modern postal and telegraphic systems for using (sic) in the country would greatly help to develop trade and commerce as well as to ensure and accelerate the dispatch of official and individual correspondence...'

The monarch appointed one prince and one high-ranking official to oversee '...the organisation of a Local Letter Post for the City of Bangkok as an experiment with a view to expanding same throughout the country.'

The first major hurdle to overcome was house numbering. Previously unknown in Bangkok, residences had to be numbered or identified in some unique way to simplify the delivery of mail.

There was also a problem of public resistance to house numbering, as many people were afraid that they would be compelled to contribute funds to the fledgling postal service. Others were worried that they would be taxed more.

The public acquiesced after the government issued a statement clarifying the aims of the new postal system, outlining the reasons for its inception, and assuring the public that they would not be subject to new or increased taxes.

With the public onside, the Department of Postal and Telegraphs was established in 1883 with Prince Bhanarungsi as Director-General. A number of Europeans were employed as officials in the initial stages to oversee the service. Thais gradually replaced them.

The main Post Office was located on the Chao Phraya River, near the mouth of the Ong Ang Canal, with a series of postage stamp shops dotted about the city and countryside serving as postal branches. In the early years there were no postal boxes and people wanting to post a letter had to go to their nearest postage stamp shop. Shopkeepers were paid four baht per month to take care of the postal box in their shop.

The postal service proved very popular and within a short time an average of 127 letters a day was being posted. In 1885, the postal service was gradually extended throughout Siam with the first up-country branch established at Samut Prakan. Others were soon set up at Bang Pa-in, Nakhon Pathom, Samut Sakhon, Samut Songkhram, Ratchaburi, and Phet Buri among others. A letter took two days to go from Bangkok to Nakhon Pathom and four days between Bangkok and Phet Buri. Parcels and registered mail were included in the system from the very beginning, although there were restrictions on certain items. For example, dynamite and other explosives were prohibited and any person found violating the law could be fined up to 800 baht.

An early postman shown on a 1976 Thai postage stamp

Communication in Siam at the time was largely conducted via waterways and bullock cart. Roads were few and the railway was still some years off. When the postal service extended to Chiang Mai, the route went up the Chao Phrya River to Nakhon Sawan, and then took a branch of the river as far as Uttaradit where it went by road through Phrae, Lampang, and Lamphun before reaching Chiang Mai. The whole process took around 15 days.

In April 1886, the postal offices located in Phuket and in the vassal state of Kedah participated in a direct exchange of mail with Penang. In the same year, direct closed mail began being sent to France and Italy. In June 1886, a line was opened between Chiang Mai and Rangoon that saw mail delivered from and to Bangkok. Mail from the north of Siam that was destined for Europe was also dispatched via Rangoon.

A mail delivery line between Bangkok and Saigon was established in March 1887 while in June 1888, an agreement was reached with the Straits Settlements for the exchange of parcels. In December 1889, the agreement was extended to include India and Britain. A similar arrangement was made with Hong Kong and this enabled correspondence to travel from Siam to Japan, Macau, and the Chinese treaty ports.

In 1890, an agreement was reached with Germany whereby parcels were sent on British steamers to London and then forwarded. A year later, German vessels began taking parcels direct to Hamburg and then dispatched throughout central Europe.

In the initial stages, the postal service focussed on overseas deliveries and receipts. One of the main reasons for this was that the average Thai person living in the interior was illiterate and therefore rarely wrote or received mail. Additionally, traders needed to maintain communication with their overseas markets, receivers, and suppliers.

Domestically, the government concluded agreements in the 1890s with the Siam Steam Navigation Company to transport mail between Bangkok and the Thai ports along the east and west coasts.

The construction and expansion of the rail network made it a viable alternative to water-borne delivery of the mail, although this didn't necessarily lead to efficiency as this extract from the *Bangkok Times* of December 1900 shows: '…when the daily service of trains was commenced to Cengkoi, residents up to the line beyond Ayuthia got their papers and letters twice a week, as often as the trains run. Since then, however, to judge by the number of complaints we are receiving, the service seems to have been reduced to once a week and not always that. Apparently the Postal Department had heard that some change was being made in the train service, and jumped to the rash conclusion that it was being reduced. At first we thought it might be unfair to complain and were willing to give the P.O. time to realize the new state of things, but complaints are still arriving that it takes a week for a paper to get up beyond Ayuthia.'

In 1905, the Postal Department arranged for the establishment of post offices at each station. A few years later, mail vans were used to collect mail from post boxes and delivered to the stations.

By 1917, with the completion of much of the rail network, the number of ports at which vessels of the Siam Steam Navigation Company were required to call was substantially cut back.

An experimental airmail service, handled by military planes, between Bangkok and Chantaburi was begun in February 1919 and proved so successful that it was expanded to Khorat, Roi-Et, and Ubon Ratchathani in 1922. Mail from Khorat to Nong Khai, which had previously taken up to 14 days, was reduced by air services to around four hours.

In 1927, the Postal Department reached an agreement with the Interior Ministry to set up a postal outlet in each district office. At this time, the postal express service was also established to circumvent theft.

Between 1927 and 1935, the postal service ran at a substantial loss, but with increased usage by the public, it had become self-sustaining by the 1970s. In 1961, Bangkok and Thonburi were divided into 12 postal districts, issued with a number, and mail collections were conducted three times a day.

In remote country areas where there was no postal outlet or the district office was some distance away, the village headman acted as postmaster. This situation has carried on into the twenty-first century in many of the remoter parts of the nation.

The construction of the Chiang Mai-Burma Road 1942-1945

Although Thailand allied itself with Japan during the Second World War, the relationship was more one of master and indentured apprentice than equals. Japanese depredations against the civilian population reflected the actions of a conqueror rather than an ally.

For example, apart from the thousands of Allied prisoners-of-war who died, many thousands of Thais also perished in the construction of the infamous Burma-Siam Railway (a.k.a. the Death Railway), carved through the inhospitable jungles of Kanchanaburi province.

Equally, Japanese soldiers would, according to the reminiscences of a Thai lady who lived in a house overlooking the railway tracks at Klong Toey, force Thais caught siphoning gasoline by way of long plastic tubes from tankers to "…drink gasoline through the same plastic tubes until they died."

To support their conquest of British-held Burma, the Japanese pressed many thousands of Thais into service to help construct a highway through the northwest of Thailand, specifically Mae Hong Son province. This engineering work, through rugged terrain, was also to cost thousands of lives (many due to malaria) and, whereas the Burma-Siam Railway was actually completed, the Burma Road (as it came to be known) was unfinished at war's end.

In the early 1990s, Highway 1095 starting just north of Chiang Mai and turning off through the small town of Pai and on to Mae Hong Son, follows the route of the planned Japanese military supply road. Although laid out by the Japanese it took almost fifty years before the road became a reality.

Just before Pai there is a disused iron bridge over the Pai River, its central steel spans bearing a plaque that reads: 'United States Steel Products Company. USA. 1930.' It would appear that, just as the central steel spans of the infamous bridge on the River Kwae were taken from Java in Indonesia, the steel for the bridge on the River Pai was appropriated from elsewhere in Japan's Greater East Asia Co-Prosperity Sphere, more than likely the occupied American colony of the Philippines. The Japanese also constructed a small airstrip in Pai, which was possibly used to supply materiel for the road building.

In the village of Pha Bong, a few kilometres beyond Mae Hong Son, are hot springs which were developed by the Japanese army as they oversaw the tediously slow construction of their supply road. Photographs taken at the time show Japanese troops tending elephants which were allegedly treated better than the labourers in that they were given alternate days off.

On 23 September 1943 the Japanese ambassador to Thailand, Tsubokami met with Prime Minister Pibul Songgram and requested an additional 20.4 million baht in funds to cover the cost of the construction of the Chiang Mai-Burma road. Its completion was considered pivotal to Japanese plans for re-supplying their forces in an offensive against the British in northeastern India.

Whether the failure to complete the road in part led to the Japanese defeat in the Imphal campaign is moot. The campaign, begun in March 1944, was aimed at capturing the twin towns of Imphal and Kohima and taking the British stores. When the British refused to retreat, the start of the monsoon season forced the Japanese into an orderly, but costly, retreat. That the Chiang Mai-Burma Road was still not much more than a forest cutting meant re-supply to the Japanese troops was perilously slow.

After the British, especially the Fourteenth Army under General (later Sir) William Slim, smashed the Japanese in a series of engagements in northern and central Burma, the remnants began a disorderly retreat back into Thailand via both the Burma-Siam Railway and the still uncompleted Chiang Mai-Burma Road.

Japanese civilians, left to fend for themselves in Rangoon, evacuated as best they could and made their way via the Three Pagodas Pass into Kanchanaburi and thence to Bangkok. Up to 30 percent died en-route and the survivors were starving when they reached the Thai capital.

In the north, many Japanese soldiers, reduced to rags and starving, were forced to sell what equipment and personal belongings they had to buy food or simply begged from local villagers. Their trucks had long since broken down or run out of fuel and the soldiers were forced to pull their equipment in oxcarts or simply carry what they could.

A British officer supervises Japanese prisoners in Bangkok

It has been suggested over 12,000 Japanese troops were killed by Karen fighters, organized and supplied by the British Special Operations Executive (SOE), as they attempted to retreat through the jungles and hills of northern Burma and Thailand. Certainly, in the early 1990s, a mass grave containing the bodies of massacred Japanese soldiers was unearthed at the town of Ban Sala Mae Noi, a village located on a bend in the Pai River. The Karen had little love for the Japanese, who had forced many locals to work as porters in support of their 1942 invasion of Burma. Those soldiers who made it as far as Chiang Mai were interned in a number of temples at the end of the war.

The April Fool's Day Coup

The 13th Constitution, officially promulgated on 22 December 1978, allowed for the prime minister and members of the cabinet to not necessarily be elected members of parliament.

It was this provision which enabled General Prem Tinsulanonda, the army commander since October 1978 and defence minister since May 1979, to be sworn in as prime minister on 3 March 1980, succeeding the out-of-favour General Kriangsak Chomanand.

Prem Tinsulanonda, Prime Minister of Thailand 1980-1988
Credit Government of Thailand derivative work: Sodacan CC BY 2.0
https://commons.wikimedia.org/w/index.php?curid=9447573

General Prem was viewed as the perfect choice to lead Thailand to a better future. With Vietnam perceived as a threat, following their invasion and overthrow of the Pol Pot regime in Cambodia, and with the Communist Party of Thailand (CPT) still active in various regions, Prem's non-elected status did not really upset the majority of Thai people.

Although a professional soldier, the 59-year-old Prem's undoubted abilities in dealing with civil problems, made him a favourite with the palace.

This close connection with the ruling dynasty would prove invaluable when Prem's first real test of power came 13 months later.

Although a firm, disciplined leader with no taint of corruption or whispers of unusual wealth about him, Prem did appear to be concentrating a substantial amount of power about his person by retaining his positions of defence minister and army commander.

Holding a political post (prime minister) while also being a senior civil servant (army commander) had been one of the reforms of the mid-1970s, designed to prevent the rise of yet another dictator. Yet Prem was subjected to mute criticism over his positions, with many believing he would retire as army commander in October 1980, when he reached the age of 60.

In late August, General Arthit Kamlang-ek and a number of other senior officers asked the palace to approve a postponement of Prem's retirement as army commander for a further 12 months.

It is suggested that General Arthit was aiming to succeed Prem and prevent the appointment of his senior rival General Sant Chitpatima, the deputy army commander, to the top post.

Although it attracted internal as well as external criticism, Prem was granted a 12-month extension to his term as army commander. The move would sow the seeds of yet another attempted military coup.

One of those most vocal in his criticism of the extension was Democratic Party leader Chuan Leekpai. Some students staged small protests, but these quickly fizzled out when the Red Guar's leader Sudsai Hasdin made oblique public threats.

A clique known as the Young Turks, middle-ranking army officers who all graduated from Chulachomklao Military Academy in 1960 and were opposed to General Arthit, also voiced opposition to the extension. The Young Turks were primarily led by Colonel's Manoon Roopkachorn, his brother Manas, and Chamlong Srimaung.

While Prem could point to significant success in accelerating the collapse of the CPT insurgency, noting the literally thousands of guerrillas emerging from the jungles and surrendering to the government, the economy itself was in recession.

This led to rumblings of discontent from within the ruling coalition, with some political leaders upset they were not benefitting in the time-honoured way for supporting Prem. The usual corruption scandals which are the bane of almost every Thai government also weakened Prem's hold on power.

The final straw for many was when it was announced, early in 1981, that Prem would seek yet a further extension as army commander. A number of ministers resigned and Kukrit Pramoj - who had hoped to succeed Kriangsak as prime minister ahead of Prem - pulled his party out of the ruling coalition in protest.

Prem reacted by forming a new coalition and appointing Sudsai Hasdin and a senior general to the cabinet. These actions provoked fears of a return to the extreme right in Thai politics.

The actual sequence of events which led to the attempted coup are still debated among some Thai history scholars.

It is believed the coup itself was not meant to remove Prem, but aimed at scything away the many allegedly corrupt and venal military men who were supporting him in the parliament. Included among these was the deputy prime minister General Pramarn Adireksarn.

The Young Turks were also angry at the appointment of corrupt, but politically adept, officers into major military positions ahead of more senior and deserving men.

Two of the coup leaders, General Sant Chitpatima and Colonel Manoon Roopkachorn, approached Prem on 31 March and asked him to prorogue parliament, suspend the constitution, and take control of the government.

There are claims Prem agreed, and the coup leaders marshaled their forces in Bangkok to aid in the takeover.

It is then alleged Prem was pressured into reneging on the idea. Despite this, the Young Turks, mostly veterans of the armed conflicts in Laos and Vietnam who considered themselves true soldiers, determined to go ahead with the coup.

On the morning of 1 April, Bangkokians awoke to find troops and tanks on the streets and tuned their radios to listen to the almost familiar strains of martial music and military announcements declaring a new government and the forced removal of the old.

The takeover was bloodless with General Sant telling the nation he was head of a Revolutionary Council. Sant stated they had abrogated the constitution, dissolved the Senate and the House of Representatives, and dismissed the cabinet.

Sant said, 'The Council detests the unseemly snatching of benefits by different groups, whoever has the longest reach seizing more profits. The bureaucracy has been allowed to deteriorate with widespread corruption, overstaffing and red tape, which caused the deserving public to suffer.'

He added the new leadership would 'eliminate the state of lawlessness and internal unrest and disorder which has disrupted political, economic, and social development.'

General Sant claimed general elections would take place as soon as the political situation was stabilized.

It is suggested Prem was initially placed under house arrest, but released after a request from the palace. Whether this is correct or not, Prem certainly organized for the royal family to be flown by helicopter to the Second Military Region headquarters in Nakhon Ratchasima, where General Arthit was deputy commander.

While Radio Thailand made intermittent announcements regarding appointments of new officials, on the afternoon of 1 April, Prem made a radio broadcast informing the coup leaders the royal family was with him.

The coup leaders shot back with claims Prem had 'abducted' the royal family.

For almost two days Prem and others negotiated with two of the four regional army commanders in an effort to secure their support. Both eventually agreed to throw their weight behind Prem and General Arthit.

While this lobbying was taking place, the Young Turks, desperate to regain the initiative, announced they had a list of 500 capitalists, most of them of Chinese origin, and they intended to purge them once they had secured power.

The Young Turks hoped to draw support from the Left and called on the labour unions to mass in Sanam Luang. The move failed, and, with only one army commander on side, the coup fell apart.

On the morning of 3 April several thousand troops loyal to Prem entered Bangkok, 55 hours after the coup had begun.

Shortly afterwards, two coup commanders, General Thongtoem Popsuk and Colonel Prachak Sawangchit surrendered to Prem's army.

Although barely a shot had been fired during the coup, one Young Turk was killed and another wounded after refusing to lay down their arms. One civilian was killed and two wounded after being caught in crossfire.

General Sant fled into exile in Burma and Prem ordered the banks to freeze his assets. His residence was turned over to General Arthit, the new First Army Region commander.

On 8 April, the governor of Bangkok, Chaowas Sudlabba, his deputy, and 50 military, police, civil servants and others were arrested and charged with complicity in the coup.

On 5 May, in keeping with the tradition of previous attempts at changing governments by force, a royal amnesty was issued to almost all those involved in the 1 April coup.

King Bhumibol Adulyadej used the anniversary of his coronation to announce an amnesty for 52 people directly involved with the failed coup. General Sant was still in exile and did not receive the royal pardon. Nor did another seven suspects who were still at large.

Deputy prime minister General Pramarn said many who had been involved in the coup had previously been loyal and 'It will be regrettable if their value is wasted.'

Around 30 of the pardoned presented themselves in front of Prem's residence to apologise in person. Prem reportedly uttered only two words to them: 'thank you'.

On 22 June, General Sant finally returned from self-imposed exile in Burma. He refused to speak about the attempted coup but would only say he was not interested in entering politics.

Of those who were not granted amnesty, including General Sant, none were ever brought up on charges relating to the attempted coup.

The coup did have the effect of stopping Prem extending his command of the army by yet another year.

Even so, there were those who resented the quashing of the revolt and both Prem and Arthit faced more than one attempt at assassination in succeeding months, with disgruntled army men claimed as the probable culprits.

General Arthit eventually became army commander in October 1982 and then supreme commander in October 1983, but retaining his commander of the army position as well.

Arthit was viewed as a serious successor to Prem, but the pair eventually fell out and in 1986 he was unceremoniously removed as supreme commander. He entered politics and led a small party into coalition with Chatichai Choonhavan in the early 1990s, even being appointed a deputy prime minister.

General Prem remained as an unelected prime minister until August 1988, a term of almost eight and a half years.

From Siam to Thailand and back again: 1939-1949

On 11 May 1939 (or 5 June according to some sources), the government of Siam, led by its nationalistic prime minister, Pibul Songgram, officially changed the name of the country to Thailand. The name means 'land of the free'.

It was also understood the name change reflected a desire by Pibul Songgram and others of like mind to eventually bring people such as the Lao, Shan and even the Khmer under Bangkok's rule.

A few months later saw the start of the Second World War. Seven days after the German invasion of Poland (1 September) and five days after the British and French declaration of war on Germany, the Thai government announced it would remain neutral.

On 12 June 1940, a treaty of friendship was signed between Thailand and Japan in Tokyo. Not putting all their eggs in one basket, Pibul Songgram's government also signed treaties of non-aggression with Britain and France in Bangkok on the same day. Of course, no one was under any illusion about the true value of any of these treaties. As with the Russo-German 10-year non-aggression pact signed between Hitler and Stalin in 1939, they weren't worth the paper they were written on.

The Japanese Fifteenth Army invaded Thailand at nine separate points on 8 December 1941, but after just five hours of resistance, Pibul Songgram ordered a cease-fire and gave permission for the Japanese to travel unhindered through the country. On 21 December, the government signed a 10-year treaty of alliance with Japan.

Then, on 25 January 1942, Thailand, honouring its alliance with Japan, declared war on Britain and the United States. On the same day, South Africa and New Zealand, supporting Britain, declared war on Thailand. Australia followed suit a few months later.

There are conflicting accounts regarding the actions of Seni Pramoj, the Thai ambassador to the United States, and his delivery of the formal declaration of war to the Americans. Some accounts claim Seni simply placed the declaration in a desk drawer and 'forgot' to deliver it. Of course everyone was aware of its existence, but by not delivering the paper it meant the two nations were not 'officially' at war. Seni claimed he went to the United States Secretary of State Cordell Hull and reluctantly delivered the declaration of war. Hull placed the parchment in a drawer and thus, by not reciprocating, Thailand and the United States were not 'officially' at war.

Seni Pramoj in 1964

Instead, Seni Pramoj set about organising what became known as the Free Thai Movement (a group of dissidents composed mainly of the elite of society, supported by the regent Pridi Banomyong).
In 1945, James Byrnes, the new Secretary of State, said because the declaration of war had never been delivered and was not in accordance with the wishes of the Thai people, the United States

ignored it and so the two nations were never officially engaged in hostilities.

In a somewhat symbolic but nonetheless significant gesture, the Allies reverted to calling Thailand by its former appellation of Siam. They were encouraged in this by Seni and the Free Thai Movement (Seri Thai) who claimed that as Thailand was effectively, if not overtly, under Japanese occupation, the nation was hardly the 'land of the free'.

By July 1944 it was clear Japan was going to lose the war and on the 24th, Pibul Songgram was forced to resign as prime minister by the National Assembly. He was replaced by Khuang Aphaiwong.
Japan surrendered on 14 August. Two days later, a broadcast from Bangkok announced Thailand had withdrawn her declaration of war against Britain, the United States and their allies and would return ceded Malay and Burmese territories.

On 8 September, Seni Pramoj and the Thai legation in Washington DC, announced that despite the end of the war and the end of the ill-fated alliance with Japan, the designation for the nation abroad would remain Siam and not Thailand. Internally, the country would continue to be called Thailand.

On 1 January 1946, a treaty of peace was signed with Britain in Singapore. As part of its punishment, Thailand was compelled to supply rice at fixed low prices to the rest of Southeast Asia for a period of time. Additionally, its internationally recognised name would remain Siam and not Thailand. A preliminary peace agreement was also signed with Australia. A final peace treaty was signed on 10 April.

It took until January 1951 before agreement was reached between Thailand and Britain, Australia, and India on an amount to be paid as war compensation.

On 16 December 1946, Siam was admitted as a member of the United Nations General Assembly.

Politically, Siam underwent a period of turmoil after the January 1948 national elections with Pibul Songgram returning to centre stage as prime minister in April after threatening the government of three-time premier Khuang Aphaiwong with military force.

Finally, on 11 May 1949, 10 years after his first attempt, Pibul Songgram again officially changed the name of the country from Siam to Thailand by decree. This action was criticised in some quarters as being undemocratic and, because the Regent had not been consulted beforehand, as disrespectful to the King. Nevertheless, the nation has been known as Thailand ever since 1949.

Monarch abdicates and takes a swipe at an unelected government

Just under three years after the coup of June 1932, King Prajadhipok (Rama VII) abdicated.

The abdication was announced on 2 March 1935. The monarch had become increasingly unhappy with the way Siam was being run by the successful coup leaders.

Just over a week after his abdication, *TIME* magazine ran a feature on the announcement, beginning with a statement most long-time expats can relate to, even in the 21st century: *'The difference between a Siamese and anybody else is that the Siamese takes things more easily...With the sublime vagueness of the true Siamese, His Majesty addressed his abdication to nobody, not to his Government which wished to keep him on the Throne, not to his people who have ever idolized him, finally not even to his Buddhist Gods.'*

King Prajadhipok and his consort had been living in England for almost a year. What must surely have made the locals a little suspicious was the pair were using the pseudonym James J. Walker (hardly an Asian-sounding cognomen) while renting a country estate called Knowle House.

Summoning the press to Knowle House on 2 March 1935 was His Majesty's youthful secretary, who announced the abdication. Part of the statement of abdication read:

When Phya Bahol and his associates seized power by military force on June 24, 1932, they invited me to remain as a constitutional king. I accepted the invitation on the understanding that Bahol and his associates would establish a constitution on the same lines as in all other countries with constitutional governments of that kind so the people would have a right to have a voice in administration and in matters of policy affecting the welfare of the people.

Owing to the fact that the promoters did not implement true political liberty to the people and the people had no opportunity of voicing their opinion before an important policy was undertaken, revolt broke out, involving civil war. When I asked that the Constitution should be changed to conform to true democracy in order to satisfy the people, the Government and its party, which now hold complete power in their hands, refused. . . . I am unable to agree that any party should carry on an administration in this way under cover of my name. . .

I hereby renounce all the rights I had been asking, but reserve all the rights I formerly enjoyed before my accession to the throne. I have no wish to exercise my right under the Succession Act to nominate my successor. I have no wish that any one should create any disturbance in the country on my behalf; if any one should use my name in this connection it must be understood that it would be without my agreement, approval or support My deepest regret is that I no longer will be able to serve my people and my country. . . . I can but pray that Siam may have prosperity and that the Siamese people may have happiness.

1934 King Prajadhipok and Queen Rambhai Barni with British PM Ramsay MacDonald at Number 10 Downing Street

As a reigning monarch, King Prajadhipok could never be interviewed. Having abdicated, his secretary agreed to let the throng of journalists onto the front lawn to ask the former Rama VII a few questions. According to the *TIME* correspondent, the now former

King Prajadhipok was quoted as saying, "One thing I want to ask you…in what you are writing about me, please do not talk about the 'brother of the moon' or the 'twenty-four umbrellas.' I am not the moon's brother. That is all bunk. There is a nine-tiered umbrella in our Siamese ritual, but I have no idea who invented the titles usually ascribed to me. . ."

From Siam, the government sent emissaries to Lausanne in Switzerland to offer the throne to Prajadhipok's 11-year-old nephew, Prince Ananda Mahidol. He would become King Rama VIII, although his mother was quoted as saying, "My son will accept the Throne of his country, if the Government does not require his presence in Siam until his health improves."

The former King Prajadhipok lived out the remainder of his life in his beloved England, dying at the age of just 48 on 30 May 1941, at the height of the Second World War.

Prince Wan: Diplomat and Philologist

In 1991 the United Nations Educational, Scientific and Cultural Organisation (UNESCO) listed Prince Wan Waithayakon Krommun Naradhip Bongs-praband- better known simply as Prince Wan - as one of the great personalities of the world in the categories of diplomat and scholar.

Prince Wan Waithayakon

It was a singular honour for a man who had dedicated his life to the service of his country and who was also responsible for coining a vast number of Thai words still in current usage.

Prince Wan, a direct descendant of King Rama IV, was born on 25 August 1891 in Bangkok. After early education at Suan Kularb School and King's College, he was awarded a King's Scholarship and in 1905 went to study in England.

An outstanding student, he collected some 17 prizes over the next five years. Attending Oxford, he majored in history and after graduating he went to Paris to study diplomacy.

His career commenced in 1917 when he was appointed Third Secretary at the embassy in Paris. In 1919, he returned to Bangkok and worked at the Foreign Office under Foreign Minister, Prince Devawongse and was also made an Adviser to King Rama VI.

In 1924, he became Under-Secretary for Foreign Affairs while in 1926 he returned to Europe as Minister accredited to Great Britain, the Netherlands and Belgium. At the same time he was appointed head of the delegation to the League of Nations. Prince Wan returned home in 1930, accepting a seat on the Faculty of Arts at Chulalongkorn University.

Just two years later, the country was thrown into political turmoil by the overthrow of the absolute monarchy. It was at this time that Prince Wan became an active philologist and over the next 44 years he was to bequeath to the Thai language around 300 words, including 'association', 'bank', 'company', 'family', 'service', 'supply', 'demand', 'freedom', 'pollution', 'revolution', 'reform', 'war' and 'zone'. Although he had an interest in playing golf and ballroom dancing, books and writing were his lifetime passion, the bibliophile amassing a large collection during his life.

Prince Wan saw the 1932 revolution as, "not just a change of government but a fundamental change in the way of life of the Thai people..." He wanted to give the revolution a reasoned voice and so he began a newspaper, the Prachachat.

In February 1941, Prince Wan was appointed to head the delegation to Tokyo to negotiate a peace treaty between Thailand and the Vichy French government of Indochina in the undeclared war that had broken out a few months before. The negotiations proved difficult and it wasn't until early March that an agreement acceptable to both sides was hammered out. Even then, Prince Wan felt the agreement was less than favourable to Thailand.

He participated in the negotiations that led to Thailand's admission to the United Nations in December 1946 and in 1947 Prince Wan was appointed Ambassador to the United States as well as Ambassador to the United Nations. Finally, in March 1952, he was appointed Foreign Minister.

In September 1954, the Southeast Asia Treaty Organisation (SEATO) was formed at a meeting in Manila in the Philippines. Aimed at providing defence for the region it consisted of the United States, Britain, Australia, New Zealand, France, Pakistan, the Philippines and Thailand.

During the delicate negotiations the work of Prince Wan was singled out for praise by British Foreign Secretary (later Prime Minister) Sir Anthony Eden who wrote, 'Your smooth and timely but firm guidance has had an essential part in the success for the work we have done.'

In April 1955, Prince Wan attended the nine-day Bandung Conference in Indonesia. Chaired by Indonesian President Sukarno, delegates from 29 Asian and African countries heard speeches denouncing colonialism and demanding self-determination for all subjugated peoples. The dignitaries included Zhou En-Lai (China), 'Pandit' Nehru (India), Prince Norodom Sihanouk (Cambodia) and Pham Van Dong (North Vietnam). Prince Wan, already noted for his tact and impartiality, was elected Rapporteur.

Prince Wan's international standing was so high that he was unanimously elected as President of the United Nations General Assembly in 1956. He held the post until 1957. Prince Wan is the only Thai to have been elevated to such a prominent position on the international stage.

During his Presidency, Prince Wan had to weather the international storm of two potentially explosive dramas: the Russian invasion of Hungary and the Suez Crisis. Both occurred in mid to late 1956, and led to fears of yet another world war. That neither incident escalated into a major conflagration was due in no small measure to the conciliatory efforts of Prince Wan.

He remained Foreign Minister (with a break of eight months in 1957) until October 1958 when he retired from international diplomacy, returning to Thailand to concentrate on linguistics and academic pursuits.

In 1969, aged 78, the elder statesman was appointed Deputy Prime Minister in the Thanom Kittikachorn government.

During his extensive public career he was President of the Royal Institute (1934-1947 and 1973-1976), President of the Siam Society (1944-1949 and 1969-1976), Rector of Thammasat University (1965-1970) and in 1946 was elected as the foundation President of the Chulalongkorn University Alumni Association. In 1971, the King appointed him President of the National Congress, the forerunner to the Legislative Assembly that eventually drafted the 1974 Constitution.

Prince Wan died on 5 September 1976, at the venerable age of 85.

The Thai invasion and occupation of the Shan States, 1942-1945

Although Thailand under Prime Minister Pibul Songgram had allied itself with the Japanese Empire, the military had not been given any major role to play in Japan's invasion of either the Malay Peninsula or Burma. Instead, the Thai army had merely been sent to the border regions to act as a reserve.

For Pibul the Japanese attitude revealed quite clearly they regarded Thailand as something less than a reliable ally. The Thai leader had wanted to be included in the invasion of Burma so he could lay claim to two areas he considered part of greater Thailand.

The first was the Tenasserim region, a strip of land on the Andaman Sea coast in southern Burma, which had been under Thai control during the Ayutthaya period (1350-1767). The second was the mountainous Shan States in northeastern Burma, populated by people ethnically related to the Thais.

Only after pressing his claims, and with the conquest of Burma almost complete, did the Japanese give Pibul permission to move, and then only into the Shan States. The Thais were tasked with engaging the Chinese (Kuomintang) 93rd Division which had moved into the area from Yunnan province in order to protect the supply routes between Rangoon and Chungking.

On 3 May 1942, the Thai air force attacked the main centre of Kengtung -close to the Sino-Burmese border- with more than 20 planes, bombing the central market. On 10 May 1942 the Northern Army, consisting of three divisions under the overall command of General Seri Roengrit and totalling around 35,000 men, crossed the Burmese border and invaded the Shan States. General Phin Choonhavan was given command of the Thai infantry.

The Thai army moved quickly and on 26 May occupied Kengtung, the Chinese retreating into the surrounding hills. The Thais established their headquarters here and certain high-ranking elements began to involve themselves in the profitable opium trade, both the locally grown and Chinese imported varieties. Within a few months the Thai Opium Monopoly based in Bangkok had imported around 36 tons of opium from the Shan States.

The political connections made at the time would later bind this mountainous region into what has become known throughout the world as the Golden Triangle. Many major Thai military personnel who came to dominate the nation's politics after the Second World War were veterans of the occupation of the Shan States, among them the-then Lieutenant Chatichai Choonhaven, Prime Minister between 1988 and 1991.

Lieutenant Chatichai Choonhaven

Unfortunately, the Thai army had been poorly equipped for the invasion and soon more soldiers were dying from mosquito-borne diseases than from enemy action. Food and medical supplies were also in short supply, making life for the average soldier quite miserable.

When Pibul visited the occupied region in February 1943, he was alarmed at the parlous state of his army and sent orders for money, supplies, and medical equipment to be sent from Bangkok to Kengtung.

On 2 February, American fighter planes had destroyed seven Thai planes on the ground at Kengtung. A month later, another raid saw one Thai plane destroyed on the ground.

By this time Pibul had become disillusioned with the Japanese alliance, and on this visit he made his first secret move to contact the Allies by sending representatives of the Thai forces occupying the Shan States to begin negotiations with the Kuomintang (Nationalist) Chinese in Yunnan.

The Japanese, for their part, recognised the fact that as Germany was slowly being beaten in the West, their own military position was also being eroded under Allied counter-attacks and they would have to honour their undertakings and grant as much of the territory Thailand sought as possible.

To this end, the conquest of the Shan States was enshrined by a treaty signed in August 1943. Thailand was granted the two easternmost Shan States, re-naming the territory the United Thai State and General Phin Choonhavan was appointed Governor. Although this did not please the Burmese, who were also about to receive a form of independence under the Japanese umbrella, the Japanese argued the British had administered the Shan States separately from Burma and the Shans were ethnically closer to the Thais than the Burmese.

At the same time, although Thailand desired the return of certain territory in Laos and Cambodia, the Japanese alliance with the Vichy French meant this could not be fulfilled. Japan instead returned control of the four Malay states of Kelantan, Kedah, Perlis and Terengganu (ceded to the British in 1909) to Thailand.

In reality, with the British going onto the offensive in western Burma and the Americans moving steadily across the Pacific, Japanese hegemony was crumbling with every new day. Leading Thai politicians realised, as did the Prime Minister, they had allied themselves with the wrong side and in July 1944 Pibul Songgram was forced to resign. The new regime, aware the Allies- and the British in particular- were keen to punish Thailand severely for its alliance with Japan, made it clear they would renounce all claims to the Shan and the Malay states once hostilities ceased.

Nevertheless, the Thai occupation of the Shan States continued until the end of the war in August 1945. Although the vast majority of Thai troops returned home after the war, a few remained to marry with the locals, settling down in the Shan States.

The Grand Palace Coup

It began on the weekend of 26-27 February 1949. Siamese naval units hostile to the Pibul Songgram government assembled in the grounds of Thammasat University before advancing on, and seizing, the nearby Grand Palace.

Although the rebellion was led on the ground by Vice-Admiral Luang Sangwon Suvanachib, a former police chief, the chief instigator was former regent and prime minister Pridi Banomyong.

Pridi Banomyong in 1947

Pridi had fled Siam after the failed 1947 coup. After growing a moustache in an effort to disguise his identity, Pridi slipped back into Siam from China in February 1949. Among the catalysts for Pridi's return from self-imposed exile and attempt to overthrow Pibul's government was the removal of the relatively neutral Khuang Aphaiwong as prime minister in April 1948. Khuang had allegedly been confronted by a number of senior military generals who demanded his resignation in favour of Pibul. Khuang resigned, but embarrassed Pibul by writing a letter claiming he had done so at gunpoint and naming the generals involved.

This act ushered in what would eventually become a quarter of a century of unchallenged military rule.

Pibul, who was still considered a war criminal by many officials in Britain and the United States left Khuang's cabinet virtually unchanged and gave orders for a new constitution to be drawn up. That constitution was passed in January 1949.

Relying on his not inconsiderable support, Pridi put his plans for a return to power into action. He considered the occupation of the Grand Palace as well as taking over the usual sources of communication (chiefly the radio stations) were essential to a successful coup.

Pridi's supporters were able to arm themselves from caches hidden since the days of the Free Thai Movement of the Second World War.

After occupying the Grand Palace and a radio station an announcement was broadcast claiming the government of Pibul Songgram had resigned and been replaced with Direck Jayanama (Direk Chaiyanam), the former Siamese ambassador to the United Kingdom, as prime minister.

Pibul had the full support of the army and he quickly marshaled his troops. They cut the signal from the occupied radio station and launched attacks designed to regain control of the facility.

Heavy fighting took place near the radio station and around the Grand Palace as the army attempted to force the naval units to either surrender or retreat.

By the morning of 27 February the radio station was back in Pibul's hands. It went back on the air to announce the failure of the rebellion.

In all, seven military personnel were killed and 23 wounded during the attempted coup. As well, three civilians died and another 14 were wounded.

With the coup a failure, Pridi took refuge at the house of a naval ally before moving into his wife's residence in central Bangkok. A few days later he transferred to his own house in Thonburi.

On 28 February thousands of people living along the Chao Phraya River were ordered to evacuate because of what authorities claimed were 'disturbed conditions'.

A report by AAP-Reuter and published worldwide on 1 March noted, 'The Government announced that all troops had been withdrawn to barracks "to eliminate a possibility of further friction between Army and Navy units."'

Five military officers were later charged with illegal arms possession. A further 20 men were charged with so-called secret society activities. Many others fled.

There were many of his opponents, including former allies Seni and Kukrit Pramoj, who viewed Pridi's actions in 1949 as the mark of a man with a lust for power.

His supporters believed he was merely trying to restore democracy to Siam.

On 4 March four former Free Thai activists and political allies of Pridi Banomyong were shot and killed while in police custody.

The police originally claimed the four former members of parliament, three of whom had served as cabinet ministers, had been shot while attempting to escape. The story then changed and the police claimed the four had been killed by assailants who had ambushed them while they were being transported in custody.

Police claimed more than 80 shots had been fired but no policemen had been killed or wounded and all the alleged assailants escaped.

A hospital examination revealed former assistant finance minister Dr Thongplaew Cholaphum's face was battered, former assistant commerce minister Chamlong Daoruang's left leg and ribs were broken, and former MP Thawin Udon's right leg was broken. Former industry minister Thong-In Bhuriphat, along with Thawin, had served as defence counsel for suspects in the alleged murder of King Ananda Mahidol.

Pridi remained in his home in Thonburi until early August. Fearing for his safety, Pridi boarded a small boat and fled to Singapore. From there he sailed to Hong Kong where he accepted an invitation from the Communist regime in Beijing to take up exile in China. Pridi never set foot in his homeland again.

Three foreign businesses make a significant mark on Thailand's economy

Established in 1878 by German pharmacist Bernhard Grimm and the Austrian merchant Erwin Mueller, the modern monolith known as B Grimm started as a chemist shop under the name Siam Dispensary. It had a fairytale beginning because the shop was soon asked to supply the royal household.

The first Siam Dispensary, Credit B.Grimm Group, CC BY-SA 4.0 https://commons.wikimedia.org/w/index.php?curid=61292640

As Siam, or more particularly, Bangkok, expanded, Grimm and Mueller recognised the opportunities available to them to begin importing European goods, so they expanded and called the business B. Grimm and Company.

By 1900 B Grimm was a major importer of general merchandise as well as specialist goods. Due to its strong connection with the royal household, the company was awarded the Garuda emblem. Included among its imports were uniforms and swords for the Siamese military and tiles for the Temple of the Emerald Buddha.

Another pharmacist, Adolf Link, from Lubeck in Germany, arrived in Bangkok to take on the role of manager in 1903. In 1910 he became a managing partner and, four years later, purchased the company.

Siam's entry into the First World War in 1917 against Germany led to Link and his family being interned and his business confiscated. After their release in 1919, the Link's went to Germany, then returned to Siam and restarted B Grimm. By 1928 it had recovered to the extent it moved into a new head office building designed and constructed by a member of the royal family. The opening was attended by King Prajadhipok.

The Second World War didn't help. When the war ended the Link's found there was no guarantee they would be allowed to continue their business. Adolf's eldest son and heir, Herbert, and his wife Alma - a trained nurse of British and Russian descent - were placed under house arrest.

After Adolf Link died in 1949, Herbert and his younger brother Gerhard revived B Grimm, obtaining exclusive distribution rights to many well-known German brands: Siemens, Krupp, Carl Zeiss and Mercedes Benz among them.

In the 1980s Alma Link became the first foreign female to be awarded the honorific title of Khunying, because of her years of charity work.

B Grimm opened a new head office in 1995, close to the Rama IX and Srinakarind Road intersection. The company currently has one of the widest portfolios of any major corporation in Thailand. Its interests range from commercial and residential real estate, construction, energy, healthcare, and fashion: a long way from a single shop selling medicines in a sleepy backwater Asian capital.

The East Asiatic Company, or EAC, has been an integral part of the economic landscape of Thailand while its parent company in Copenhagen, Denmark has tentacles that spread across the globe in the shipping, trading and industrial sectors.

Starting as a shipping company under the auspices of Captain Hans Niels Anderson in 1884, the EAC was originally known simply as Anderson and Co. The name East Asiatic Company was adopted in 1897, after Anderson returned to Denmark.

Operating out of Copenhagen and Bangkok, the EAC grew rapidly. In Bangkok, the company was chiefly concerned with importing goods and the forestry industry. Teak and other wood was in huge demand in those *fin de siecle* days and the Bangkok branch of the EAC soon had its own sawmill.

Next it was rubber, and the company acquired rubber plantations while it opened offices in countries as diverse as Malaysia, China, South Africa, and France. Within Siam, the EAC opened branches in Hat Yai, Surat Thani, Lampang, and Chiang Mai. By this time the company was running a fleet of steamships, though in 1912 they were replaced by diesel vessels.

The EAC survived the ravages of the two World Wars and stretching into the 1960s it began supplying Canadian wheat to China.

At one stage in the 1970s the EAC was considered the biggest company in Denmark in terms of turnover. Naturally, a lot of its profits also emanated via its operations in Thailand.

Yet, when economic times became tough in the 1980s it looked for a time as though the company would be lucky to survive. Severe financial losses necessitated a restructuring alongside management changes and layoffs, but by the late 1990s the EAC was once again prospering.

Anders Normann became chairman of the Thai side of the business and in 1996 he saw the EAC register a turnover of 3.9 billion baht.

Since 2000, the EAC has expanded its distribution of industrial ingredients into the primary markets of South Asia and Southeast Asia, from India to Vietnam, Singapore, Malaysia, Indonesia, the Philippines, Cambodia, and, of course, Thailand.

Finally, the surname Leonowens will almost certainly be familiar to anyone who has visited, lived or worked in Thailand. It was, of course, made famous, or infamous, depending on your point of view, by Anna Leonowens, who was for a time a tutor at the Royal Court of King Mongkut in the mid-nineteenth century. She would become the subject of a novel, a stage play and a couple of Hollywood films, none of which have ever been greeted with much enthusiasm in Thailand.

Yet the trading company Louis T. Leonowens (Thailand) Ltd is one of the most longest-established and prosperous in Thailand, and was founded by Anna Leonowens' son in 1905.

Louis Thomas Gunnis Leonowens was born in 1856. In his mid-twenties Louis came to Siam and granted a commission, as a captain, in the cavalry. He only stayed for a few years before deciding to go into the prosperous teak trade. From this he founded the company that still bears his name.

Initially, LTL, as it is commonly known, dealt primarily with teak leases and as an agency for imported champagne, whisky, and cigars as well as cement and typewriters. Louis became less involved in the general running of his company after 1906 and he left Siam in 1913, never to return.

LTL prospered up until the Second World War. As with many other companies, it was taken over by the Japanese military in the period 1942-1945. However, by the 1950s LTL was once again well and truly back in profitable business. Its forestry lease had expired so LTL was restructured and moved into the area of general trading.

By the 1960s there were LTL offices and subsidiaries all over the region. In Thailand, LTL opened a tractor assembly plant.

In 1986 LTL became part of the Getz Group in a merger with Muller and Phipps. It then expanded to include trading in industrial products, building material and equipment. The 1997 Asian financial crisis hit the company hard and forced it to restructure.

The end result saw LTL focus more on distribution systems and improving its manufacturing and service sectors.

By the early twenty-first century the company had five divisions: Agricultural, Building and Architectural, Chemicals, Firearms, and Hardware. Products in each division are considered the best in its class. Quite a change from the teak-focussed business it was just a hundred years earlier.

The Dispute over Phra Viharn (Preah Vihear)

In 2007 the government of Cambodia approached UNESCO and proposed the 11th century Brahmanic-style Preah Vihear temple as a World Heritage Site. Known by the Thai as Khao Phra Viharn, the temple, sits atop a 525-metre high escarpment in a remote corner of the eastern section of the Dangrek mountain range on the Thai border in Sisaket province. The Cambodian action was protested by Thailand that claimed a 4.6 square kilometre area of territory close to the temple was still in dispute, despite a controversial 1962 ruling by the International Court of Justice (ICJ) awarding the temple to Cambodia.

A meeting took place between Thai and Cambodian officials at UNESCO headquarters in Paris in May 2007, ending with the Cambodians agreeing to draw a map that only included the temple.

The issue came to life again in June 2008 when Cambodia said it intended to present the redrawn map to a UNESCO meeting scheduled for July. Despite objections from some opposition members of parliament and street protests by the People's Alliance for Democracy (PAD), Prime Minister Samak Sundaravej looked set to sign Thailand's agreement to the new Cambodian map, a pre-requisite for UNESCO to consider awarding Preah Vihear World Heritage status.

PAD leader Sondhi Limthongkul alleged Foreign Minister Noppadon Pattama (a lawyer) was giving up the disputed territory to help his former client, ousted premier Thaksin Shinawatra obtain a casino concession on Koh Kong, a Cambodian island close to the Thai frontier. Whatever the truth of these allegations, the issue inflamed nationalist passions on both sides, just as it had more than four decades earlier.

On 7 July 2008 UNESCO approved Preah Vihear's World Heritage listing. Noppadon Pattama resigned the next day after the Constitution Court ruled he violated the charter by signing a joint communique on 18 June backing the Cambodian application without first obtaining parliamentary approval.

Shortly after, Thailand and Cambodia began deploying troops in and around the site. Cambodia claimed Thai soldiers were on its territory, a charge the Thais denied. Thailand accused Cambodia of allowing its citizens to establish a permanent village within the temple complex. In October, four soldiers were killed in armed clashes and in April 2009 another four, two from either side, died in a brief gun battle.

By this time Thailand had seen the removal of two prime ministers, Samak Sundaravej and Somchai Wongsawat, and the controversial installation of Abhisit Vejjajiva as premier. On the Cambodian side, Prime Minister Hun Sen, continuing an unbroken run of power stretching from December 1985, easily won general elections in July 2008.

Both governments pledged to solve the dispute with bilateral talks and a Joint Boundary Commission (JBC).

Located in an area described by a French military officer in 1907 as 'desolate' and 'despairingly monotonous', Preah Vihear first came to prominence in 1949 when it was discovered it had been occupied 'by a small group of Siamese sent by the local authorities for the purpose of guarding the Temple.'

The French, then controlling Cambodia, lodged a diplomatic protest at Bangkok asserting by virtue of the Franco-Siamese agreements concluded in 1904 and 1907 the temple was inside Cambodia.

Diplomatic protests were repeated throughout the year, but Thailand continued its occupation. After independence in 1953, Cambodia established a diplomatic mission in Thailand. On 22 January 1954, the mission protested that Cambodian guards had been forced to withdraw by Thai authorities. Cambodia informed Bangkok it intended to send troops to guard Preah Vihear. This was forestalled when Thai soldiers occupied the site.

Cambodia attempted to settle the matter in bilateral talks. Unsuccessful negotiations took place in Bangkok in 1958 and again in 1959. Cambodia then took its case to the ICJ, lodging an application in October 1959.

At the time of the Thailand *v* Cambodia case the ICJ President was Bohdan Winiarski of Poland, who, with Abdul Badawi of Egypt and Jules Basdevant of France, was an original member of the court. The Vice President was Ricardo Alfaro, a former President of Panama, who joined the ICJ in 1959, at the age of 76.

Other judges sitting on the case included 59-year-old Sir Gerald Fitzmaurice of the United Kingdom, Wellington Koo of China, and Sir Percy Spender of Australia.

Sir Gerald Fitzmaurice came to the ICJ in 1960 after a long career culminating as senior legal adviser at the British Foreign Office.

Wellington Koo became an ICJ judge in 1957, aged 69. A former President of the Republic of China, he had been an Ambassador to France, Britain, and the United States.

Sir Percy Spender joined the ICJ in 1958, aged 60, after serving as Australian Ambassador to the United States, Vice President of the UN General Assembly and Australian Foreign Minister.

Thailand named their Ambassador to the Netherlands Prince Vongsamahip Jayankura as their agent. Among those assisting him were Seni Pramoj (a former Thai Prime Minister), Sir Frank Soskice, a former British Attorney General, and Professor James Hyde of the University of Columbia Law Faculty and member of the Bar of the United States Supreme Court.

On the Cambodian side the most prominent name assisting their claim was Dean Acheson, Secretary of State under Harry Truman and member of the Bar of the United States Supreme Court.

Thailand questioned the validity of the ICJ's jurisdiction in the case. Thailand claimed while it accepted the jurisdiction of the Permanent Court of International Justice, it believed this had lapsed with the creation of the ICJ. The ICJ rejected the Thai argument, ruling it had the right to hear the case.

The first hearing date took place on 10 April 1961 with the ICJ noting the dispute originated out of the 1904-1908 boundary settlements made between Siam and France.

'The application of the Treaty of 13 February 1904...established the general character of the frontier the exact boundary of which was to be delimited by a Franco-Siamese Mixed Commission...'

According to Article 1 of the 1904 treaty, the frontier where Preah Vihear is situated was to follow 'the watershed between the basins of the Nam Sen and the Mekong, on the one hand, and the Nam Moun, on the other hand, and rejoins the Phnom Padang chain the crest of which it follows eastwards to the Mekong.'

To establish this line a meeting held in December 1906 agreed the Mixed Commission should travel along the Dangrek range with the French surveying the eastern part.

The president of the French section was Lieutenant-Colonel Fernand Bernard. An avowed colonialist, Bernard played a key part in convincing the French government to take 'advantage of the completion of the boundary work to demand [the provinces of] Battambang and Siem Reap from Siam…' This was achieved by way of the 1907 treaty.

The ICJ agreed there was no reference to the Dangrek region in any Mixed Commission meetings after 1906, but considered 'a frontier had been surveyed and fixed.'

The Thai government did not possess the technical capacity to have maps prepared, depending on the accuracy of the frontier charts, completed in 1907, 'by a team of French officers, some of whom had been members of the Mixed Commission…' Copies of these were given to Siam in 1908.

Among the charts was Annex I, 'a map of the Dangrek range showing Preah Vihear on the Cambodian side. It was on that map…Cambodia had principally relied in support of her claim to sovereignty over the Temple.'

On 15 June 1962 the ICJ found in favour of Cambodia by a vote of nine to three, compelling Thailand to withdraw from the temple grounds.

Thailand argued that since Annex I was not the work of the Mixed Commission it had no binding character because the frontier indicated on it 'was not the true watershed line… the true watershed line would place the Temple in Thailand…' Thailand claimed the map had never been accepted or, had she done so, it was only 'because of a mistaken belief that the frontier indicated corresponded with the watershed line.'

Part of the 1907 French Siamese treaty monument in Phnom Penh, Cambodia

While the ICJ accepted Annex I was not formally approved by the Mixed Commission, the majority judges believed since there had been no reaction from Thailand at the time and for years afterwards '...they must be held to have acquiesced.'

The ICJ pointed out the Thai government did not query Annex I in negotiations with Cambodia in 1958 even though in 1934 an officer of the Royal Thai Survey Department doing work along the Dangrek concluded Preah Vihear lay in Thai territory. A follow-up survey in 1937 reached the same conclusion. Until then Thailand had no reason to believe an error had been made in the dividing line with Cambodia. Despite discovering this error the judges wrote Thailand

'...continued also to use and...publish maps showing Preah Vihear as lying in Cambodia.'

The judges wondered why Thailand had not raised objections during negotiations with France over a treaty signed with France in 1937 and the 1947 Franco-Siamese Conciliation Commission held in Washington. 'The natural inference was that she had accepted the frontier at Preah Vihear as it was drawn on the map...'

For her part Thailand claimed she had been in possession of Preah Vihear and did not need to raise the matter, producing acts of her administration as evidence she never accepted the Annex I line at the temple. Thailand claimed, 'Wherever there is a cliff edge in the Dangrek the edge of the cliff is, and has been, accepted as constituting the watershed boundary established in this region by Article 1 of the...Treaty of 1904.'

The court disagreed and took the view a 1930 visit by the-then Foreign Minister Prince Damrong Rajanubhab to the temple, where he was officially received by the French Resident for the adjoining Cambodian province, as evidence of her acceptance of Annex I.

Sir Gerald Fitzmaurice noted title to territory is abandoned, '...by letting another country assume and carry out for many years all the responsibilities and expenses in connection with the territory concerned. Could anything be imagined more obviously amounting to acquiescence, that is in effect abandonment? Such a course of...inaction, disqualifies the country concerned from asserting the continued existence of the title.'

Sir Percy Spender on the other hand wrote in relation to Prince Damrong's visit, 'It is significant that the Governor of the Cambodian province adjacent to the Temple had not the slightest idea where the frontier lines were. All he appeared to know was that the Temple was, so he claimed, within Cambodian territory.'

The ICJ appear to have disregarded the turbulent history of Franco-Thai relations in the period from 1867 -when Siam surrendered Cambodia to French hegemony- until the Franco-Thai border war of 1940-1941. From the late nineteenth century until the outbreak of the First World War there was a belief that France would ultimately annex Siam. Even Britain believed this would happen.

During the 1893 Paknam crisis the British Foreign Secretary Lord Rosebery remarked to Queen Victoria: 'If the French cut the throats of half Siam in cold blood we should not be justified in going to war with them.' In a private letter written in January 1904, Francois Deloncle, a businessman, foreign service official and politician wrote of a conversation he had with Theophile Delcasse, the French Foreign Minister, about an idea 'for a deal with England by which we would give up our rights in Muscat in return for full freedom of action at Bangkok: Muscat in return for the Menam Valley.'

By a strange paradox France's entente with Britain in 1904 led to her giving up ambitions of complete annexation of Siam. Conversely, the French colonialist lobby found renewed strength in their ambition to stretch French hegemony to the Mekong River and beyond, albeit now stopping short of aiming for control of the Menam Valley. It was this French pressure that led to the 1904 and 1907 treaties, setting in train what would prove to be more than a century of border conflict.

In their final judgement it was Siam's implied acceptance of Annex I the ICJ considered crucial, suggesting Siam and France had come to a tacit agreement whereby the adoption of the map line prevailed over the provisions of the 1904 treaty. The judges felt there was no reason to think either country attached any special importance to the line of the watershed 'compared with the...importance of a final regulation of their own frontiers...'

Strangely the assenting justices considered it 'unnecessary to consider whether the line as mapped did in fact correspond to the true watershed line.'

The verdict led to street protests across Thailand, mainly led by students. The student body at Thammasat University demanded the withdrawal of an honorary degree conferred on Prince Norodom Sihanouk, Cambodia's head of state. Prince Sihanouk, who had shaved his head in accordance with a vow he made with regard to the dispute, returned the degree by way of the Indonesian embassy.

Despite the protests Thai Prime Minister Sarit Thanarat removed his forces from Preah Vihear in a ceremony that took place on 15 July 1962. Notably, the Thai flag and flagpole were taken down in a standing position, leading some observers to the conclusion the Thais were determined to come back at a later date.

The three dissenting judges, Wellington Koo, Sir Percy Spender, and Lucio Manuel Moreno Quintana of Argentina, a then 64-year-old justice appointed to the ICJ in 1955, appended their reasons for disagreeing with the majority of their peers.

Quintana made the point that since Cambodia and Thailand were able to furnish evidence of their respective and overlapping administration of the temple area the ICJ should simply have addressed what the dissenting judges believed was the central issue: 'the correct application of the 1904 Treaty…'

Sir Percy Spender noted the fact Annex I did not come into being until November 1907 is, 'a critical date since…the Mixed Commission no longer existed. [It] never met after 18 January 1907 and the topographical officers did not complete their work until at least a month later, [so] no report…and no sketch or working map in relation to the Dangrek frontier region of any description could ever have been placed before the Mixed Commission for discussion or decision.'

Spender, Koo and Quintana, felt it was presumptuous to suggest, '…the Mixed Commission must…have made a decision delimiting the Dangrek by agreeing to the frontier line shown in or in the form of Annex I…'

Cambodia contended Siam's request for French officers to draw up the frontier maps was a tacit acceptance by her of those maps as representing the border. The three dissenting judges suggested the issuance of maps by France to Siam was a separate matter and in no way binding upon Siam.

According to Spender, 'the Temple was not of any great significance to either State in 1908-1909-it never found a mention in any of the voluminous correspondence of Colonel Bernard…' He suggested the reason for this was simple: 'The Temple ruins, which were the subject of a number of scattered visits by archaeologists, were allowed to submit to the years and the elements. The region to the immediate north of the escarpment dominating the Cambodian plains was forbidding and…territory, certainly not in the early part of this century, of any great consequence to France or Thailand…'

Quintana noted, 'A well-established rule was moreover embodied in Article 29 of the Treaty of Versailles of 28 June 1919. This rule States that, when there is a discrepancy concerning a frontier delimitation between the text of a treaty and maps, it is the text and not the maps which is final…An error remains an error and cannot by repetition make good acts of later date that are based upon that error.'

He quoted an arbitrator in a previous case who said, '... only with the greatest caution can account be taken of maps in deciding a question of sovereignty...If the Arbitrator is satisfied as to the existence of legally relevant facts which contradict the statements of cartographers whose sources of information are not known, he can attach no weight to the maps…'

Thailand's expert witnesses, Professor Willem Schermerhorn and Friedrich Ackermann, of the Netherlands-based International Training Centre for Aerial Survey had conducted a survey of the disputed area and pointed out a glaring mistake in Annex I with regard to the location of a non-descript but nonetheless important stream, the O.Tasem.

As Spender noted, the mistake meant Annex I did not conform, '…with the treaty line of the watershed stipulated in Article 1 of the Treaty of 1904…' Since the O.Tasem was incorrectly located this threw, '…the frontier line shown on Annex I completely out of alignment with the line of the watershed in the region of the Temple. The result was to leave the Temple wholly within the territory of Cambodia.'

The stream passes to the south of a mountain known as Phnom Trap, a few kilometres west of Preah Vihear but Annex I, '…places the river as running around this mountain to the north of it.'

Quintana believed the court case revolved around one question: 'is the temple of Preah Vihear situated south of the line stipulated by the treaty-that is to say, in Cambodian territory-or north of it, which would put the temple in Thai territory? The decisive geographical factor…is the line of the watershed…A watershed is not an intellectual abstraction; it is the result of the characteristics of the terrain, and it is always a topographical feature- the crest of a mountain, the ridge of an escarpment or the height of a piece of land…'

By placing the O.Tasem to the north of Phnom Trap mountain, and it goes up to two kilometres at certain points, the line of the watershed on Annex I was thrown considerably north of the correct watershed line, 'attributing to Cambodia territory to which she was not entitled.'

Quintana wrote that Ackermann's topographical work firmly established the watershed line to the one submitted by Professor Schermerhorn, saying, 'Even if the alternative line had been the true line it would still not have left the temple area in Cambodian territory. And it is the question of the sovereignty over the temple that is put to the Court, and no other. The waters of a river basin may run down from a promontory like one on which the temple is situated, but they can never run up it. That is obvious.'

The Death Railway 1942-1945

The history of the Japanese invasion and conquest of much of the Southeast Asian region and the Pacific islands is not only one of an astonishing military triumph, but also of a massive logistical exercise in the movement of slave labour and prisoners of war across vast areas of the 'Greater East Asia Co-Prosperity Sphere', as the occupied areas were euphemistically called, to wherever Japan needed workers.

One of the main theatres of operation involving Thailand was the construction of a railway from Malaya to Burma via the Thai province of Kanchanaburi.

Prior to the outbreak of the Second World War a British company had investigated the feasibility of building a railway from Bangkok into the heartland of Burma. The investigators concluded the potential cost in lives because of the diseases rife in the area as well as the difficulty of construction through inhospitable terrain made the project unviable.

For the Japanese in 1942 the need to construct a railway to supply their forces campaigning in Burma as well as opening a route to India and southern China negated the apparent difficulties.

Whereas the British surveyors looked at constructing their railway line by going around hills, the Japanese decided they would go straight through. The railway would extend for some 400 kilometres through almost impenetrable jungle between Burma and Thailand.

According to one source, 'there were 4 million cubic metres of earthworks, 3 million metres of rock and almost 14 kilometres of bridgework [eventually] constructed...'

The generally accepted figure is that around 330,000 workers, including 61,000 prisoners of war, were coerced into working on the rail line. Of the 270,000 native labourers, brought from Burma, Thailand, India and Malaya, around 90,000 (33 percent) died. Few graves were dug for these forgotten slave labourers and it is certain many more died from starvation and disease long before reaching their former homes. For the Thais this was galling, as the nation was officially an ally of imperial Japan, yet countless thousands of locals died at the hands of the Japanese military.

The prisoners of war (POW's) were drawn from British, Australian and Dutch captives and some Americans. The fall of Singapore in February 1942 saw an alleged 130,000 Allied troops (this figure is disputed in some quarters) fall into the hands of the Japanese. A perfect slave labour force to build a difficult railway line.

Initially, the Japanese military in occupied Singapore informed the Australian and British commanders in Changi prison camp that they required a large force of POW's to go north by train through Malaya to work in Thailand. Stating that Changi was becoming too crowded, the Japanese claimed the selected POW's would receive good food and be housed in better facilities.

Although the British and Australian senior officers were suspicious, there was little they could do to check the veracity of the Japanese claims. Within months of the first group of POW's leaving Changi (in June 1942), the prison camp in Singapore was reduced to a few thousand men as more and more Allied prisoners were shipped north to the steaming jungles of western Thailand and eastern Burma. POW's were also sent from camps on Java, Sumatra, and Borneo.

Fortunately, because of their suspicions, the British and Australian commanders made sure the troops going north were accompanied by as many medical men and medicines as possible. This act alone helped save the lives of countless numbers of POW's.

There were two sections of the railway, one in Burma and one in Thailand, the pair separated by the Three Pagodas Pass. According to one Australian prisoner, 'This Pass was a sort of watershed that made all the difference between what you died of, although the death rates were much of a muchness either side...I was on the Burma section...so we died of starvation. The men in the Siamese [Thai] section died from cholera...' Apart from starvation and cholera, the men died of beriberi, dysentery and malaria.

Originally, the Japanese considered that it would take somewhere between five and six years to complete the line from Kanchanaburi to Thanbyuzayat in Burma. This would mean having a direct line from Singapore, through Malaya and Thailand and connecting to the existing rail network in Burma. Apart from supplying their bases in Burma, the Japanese also planned to use the railway to launch an attack on India.

Given the war situation, the Japanese commanders on the ground were put under great pressure to finish the job with all haste. To this end they pushed their slave labour beyond breaking point and succeeded in completing the work in just 16 months. According to one source, a total of 688 bridges were constructed along the length of the railway. The last piece of the line was finished in mid-October 1943.

Bridge over the River Kwai by Leo Rawlings, a POW dated 1943

The construction of the bridge over the River Kwae (generally misspelt as Kwai) was particularly costly in lives, as was the building of a wooden viaduct near Nam Tok. The bridge was completed in mid-July 1943 and Japanese troop and supply trains were using the line from mid-October onwards. Thereafter the prisoners were used for maintenance and repair work following Allied bombing raids.

The Japanese refused to allow the prisoners to erect a banner (white triangle on a blue background) to indicate the presence of POW camp. The result was Allied bombing raids frequently led to casualties among the POW's. In one raid alone some 95 men were killed and over 300 wounded.

The Allies managed to destroy the bridges over the River Kwae in raids in June 1945.

The toll on human life was devastating. The railway line was constructed over the remains of approximately 16,000 Allied prisoners of war and 75,000 Asian labourers. At least one man died for every sleeper laid on the railway track

Select Bibliography

Abu Talib Ahmad, Liok Ee Tan: *New Terrains in Southeast Asian History* (Ohio University Press 2003)

Annual Register: editions 1971-1979; 1989-1994

Arnold, Peter: The Pictorial History of Boxing (Bison 1988)

Bangkok Post: Chronicle of Thailand (Editions Didier Millet & Bangkok Post 2009)

Bangkok Post: 60 Hotlists in Phuket, Krabi, Phangnga special publication (Post Publishing 2013)

Bangkok Post: The Past is Present special publication (Post Publishing 2013)

Bangkok Post: Constants, Change and Contrasts (Post Publishing 2006)

Bangkok Post: Brunch section, 8 August 2010 pp16-17

Bloodworth, Dennis: An Eye for the Dragon (Farrar, Straus and Giroux 1970)

Bonner, Raymond: Waltzing with a Dictator (Times Books 1987)

Burton, Sandra: Impossible Dream (Warner 1989)

Charlton, Peter: *War Against Japan 1941-1942* (Time-Life 1988)

Cheng, Weichung: *War, Trade and Piracy in the China Seas (1622-1683)* (Brill 2013)

Current Biography Yearbook 1970-1995 (H.H. Wilson Company)

Cruysse, Dirk Van der: *Siam & the West, 1500-1700* (Silkworm 2002)

Davis, Lee: *Man-Made Catastrophes* (Facts on File 1993)

Dennis, Peter: *Mountbatten and South East Asia Command, 1945-46* (Manchester University Press 1987)

Dictionary of Oriental Literatures, South and Southeast Asia Allen & Unwin 1974

Dupuy & Dupuy: *The Encyclopaedia of Military History* (Jane's 1976)

Dupuy, Trevor Nevitt: The Military History of World War II, Volume 16 (Franklin Watts 1965)

Edwards, Peter with Pemberton, Gregory: Crises and Commitments (Allen & Unwin 1992)

Fry, Gerald; Nieminen, Gayla; Smith, Harold: Historical Dictionary of Thailand (Scarecrow Press 2013)

Golesworthy, Maurice: Encyclopaedia of Boxing (Robert Hale 1988)
Gray, Tony: Champions of Peace (Paddington Press 1976)
Harpur, James: War Without End (Longman 1996)
Haythornthwaite, Philip: The Colonial Wars Source Book (Arms & Armour 1995)
Isaacs, Arnold, Hardy, Gordon & Brown, MacAlister: Pawns of War (Boston Publishing 1987)
Jones, Barry & Dixon, M.V.: The Macmillan Dictionary of Biography (Macmillan 1989)
Karnow, Stanley: In Our Image (Random House 1989)
Karnow, Stanley: Vietnam, A History (Viking Press 1983)
Keegan, John & Wheatcroft, Andrew: Who's Who in Military History from 1453 (Hutchinson 1987)
Keesing's Record of World Events (formerly Contemporary Archives) 1931-1970; 1981; 1983-1996
Kennedy, J.: A History of Malaya (Macmillan 1962)
Kratoska, Paul H. (editor): Southeast Asian Minorities in the Wartime Japanese Empire (Routledge 2002)
Lentz, Harris: Assassinations and Executions, An Encyclopaedia of Political Violence 1865-1986 (St James 1998)
Marrin, Albert: America and Vietnam (Viking 1992)
Mercer, Derrik, Gould, David, Heald, Henrietta et al: Chronicle of the Year 1990 (Chronicle 1990)
Mercer, Derrik, Gould, David, Heald, Henrietta et al: Chronicle of the Year 1991 (Chronicle 1991)
Moskin, Robert: The Story of the US Marine Corps (Paddington Press 1979)
Nazar, Naureen: Chronology of Conflict and Cooperation in Southeast Asia Post-Cold War Era (Area Study Centre 2006)
Reid, Anthony: Southeast Asia in the Early Modern Era (Cornell 1993)
Reynolds, Bruce E.: Thailand's Secret War (Cambridge University Press 2005)
Sagar, D. J.: Major Political Events in Indo-China 1945-1990 (Facts On File 1991)
Sato, Shigeru: War, Nationalism and Peasants (Allen & Unwin 1994)

Thak Chaloemtiarana: Thailand: The Politics of Despotic Paternalism (Cornell 2007)
The Nation: Thailand's Defining Moments and…The Future (Nation: 2007)
Tinker, Hugh: South Asia: A Short History (Macmillan 1989)
Tuchman, Barbara: Sand Against the Wind (Macmillan 1970)
Turnbull, C. Mary: A Short History of Malaysia, Singapore and Brunei (Cassell 1980)
Various (Grissarin Chungsiriwat; Nicholas Grossman): Thailand at Random (Editions Didier Millet 2012)
Williams, Neville: Chronology of the Modern World 1763-1965 (Penguin Books 1965)
Wood, W.A.R.: A History of Siam (Chalermnit Press 1924)
Wyatt, David K.: Thailand, A Short History (Yale University Press 1984)
Zeigler, Philip: Mountbatten (Collins 1985)

Index

A

B

C

D

E

F

G

H

M

N

O

P

Q

R

S

T

U